House Beautiful

READY, SET, DECORATE

House Beautiful

READY, SET, DECORATE

THE COMPLETE GUIDE TO GETTING IT RIGHT EVERY TIME

EMMA CALLERY

Hearst Books
A Division of Sterling Publishing Co., Inc.
New York

Copyright © 2006 by Hearst Communications, Inc.

Created, edited, and designed by
Duncan Baird Publishers Ltd., Castle House,
75–76 Wells Street, London W1T 3QH

Managing editor: Emma Callery
Editor: Chris Lacey
Designer: Alison Shackleton

Photographs: see credits on page 126. The publisher has made every effort to properly credit the photographers whose work appears in this book. Please let us know if an error has been made, and we will make any necessary changes in subsequent printings.

Library of Congress Cataloging-in-Publication Data

House beautiful : ready, set, decorate : the complete guide to getting it right every time / the editors of House Beautiful magazine. p. cm.
Includes index.
ISBN 1-58816-499-3
1. Dwellings—Maintenance and repair—Amateurs' manuals. 2. Dwellings—Remodeling—Amateurs' manuals. 3. Interior decoration—Amateurs' manuals. I. House beautiful.
TH4817.3.H6735 2006
747--dc22
2005018989

1 2 3 4 5 6 7 8 9 10

Published by Hearst Books
A Division of Sterling Publishing Co., Inc.
387 Park Avenue South, New York, NY 10016

House Beautiful and Hearst Books are trademarks of Hearst Communications, Inc.

www.housebeautiful.com

For information about custom editions, special sales, premium and corporate purchases, please contact Sterling Special Sales Department at 800-805-5489 or specialsales@sterlingpub.com

Distributed in Canada by Sterling Publishing
c/o Canadian Manda Group,
165 Dufferin Street, Toronto, Ontario, Canada M6K 3H6

Distributed in Australia by Capricorn Link (Australia) Pty. Ltd.,
P. O. Box 704, Windsor, NSW 2756 Australia

Manufactured in China
Sterling ISBN 13: 978-1-58816-499-5
ISBN 10: 1-58816-499-3

CONTENTS

Introduction

As the saying goes, home is where the heart is, and in these times when we all lead increasingly busy lives, home is our refuge from the hectic world outside. So we want it to be comfortable, to be a nice place to just be and to match our character so it feels like home, not merely a house.

Few things can be as rewarding as having a hand in transforming your own home so that it reflects you and the people who live in it with you. You might want a unified, consistent look that shows you are in control. Maybe you dream of every room having a different character and chance to sparkle in its own way. Perhaps you are proud of your home's architectural features and want to show them in their best light.

It is possible to transform your home into something you are excited about and where you love to be, where every room has its own look and atmosphere. The transformation won't happen overnight, but it needn't take forever, either. Every room you change is like climbing a ladder, in which each step is a new skill or insight. When you get to the top of that ladder, you'll have created something you are proud of, and you'll have the confidence to shift that ladder into the next room and start all over again, knowing you can move up those steps a little bit faster.

This book can help you climb the skills ladder. It starts by looking at painting (pages 8–21), probably the quickest way in which you can totally change the look of a room. You'll find advice on devising a color scheme, the vital skills of preparation to make sure your paintwork looks great for years, and how to paint like a professional.

Of course, an alternative to painting a wall is to paper it, and the following section (pages 22–33) gives you the low-down on the types of wall coverings available, and how to get them on the wall. Then, still working with walls, we take a look at the choices of tiles available, and techniques for doing your own tiling and creating your own effects (pages 34–45).

After that, there is a larger chapter about flooring, which looks at the wide range of flooring types on the market, and which ones you could cope with fitting yourself (pages 46–61).

Kitchens and bathrooms always represent a large investment if you are installing or updating one (pages 62–75). So it's important to consider all the basics, whether you're choosing a completely new kitchen or perhaps just considering replacing some of the doors. If it's the bathroom you are looking at, the options that are available to you are helpfully broken down in this particular chapter.

Once the shell of the room is right, it's time to turn to the finer details, such as soft furnishings, which offer you the chance to refine your decorating scheme with some great individual touches (pages 76–81). *Ready, Set, Decorate* also studies the wide range of window treatments to choose from, showing you just how to make the most of your windows whether they are big or small (pages 88–103).

Storage is the next topic (pages 104–113), with advice on how to keep your transformed home free of clutter, because everything has its place, with the attractive items on show and mundane but useful objects easily at hand. Finally, there is a briefing on lighting (pages 114–125), which can have such an impact on how good a room looks after sunset.

To help you get the most out of the information in this book each of these chapters is broken down into three sections. The first, "Ready," provides a thorough background briefing on the choices you need to make as you plan what you would like to do and what is possible. This will advise you on the materials you will need, and give an overview of the subject. The second section is called "Set" and deals with preparation for the job: what equipment is required, and the vital process of getting everything ready so your work looks good for years, not months. Finally, the "Decorate" section takes you to the final finish, looking at the techniques you will be using and helping you stay organized so that jobs happen in the right order. Equipped with an overview, planning, and detailed advice on how to do the job, there's nothing to stop you now!

▶ Painting the woodwork in a contrasting color to the rest of the room provides interest and an opportunity for exploring different color combinations.

PAGES 18–19 FOR USING GLOSS PAINT

▶ Paint walls with a single color or look to a paint technique for a more unusual finish.

PAGE 13 FOR PAINT FINISHES

▶ Painted surfaces needn't be limited to ceilings, walls, and floors—furniture responds well to a touch of paint too.

PAGES 14–15 FOR PREPARATION

▶ Enjoy choosing your color scheme: harmonizing and complementary colors introduce interest to a room.

PAGES 10–11 FOR COLOR STYLING

PAINTING

Painting a room changes its character,
and if you decide you don't like this new
persona, you can easily alter it again.
Painting is the easiest of the decorating
skills for an amateur to master.

Ready?

The joy of using paint is that, given well-prepared walls, it makes for a quick and inexpensive transformation. Furthermore, the colors can be changed as frequently as you like. The tips on color styling below will guide you, but be courageous and follow your instincts: choose a color you love and base the room around it, opting for harmonizing colors (which are neighbors on the color wheel—see opposite), or contrasting colors (opposites on the wheel), or a blend of all three, but not in the same proportions. Bearing in mind that colors set moods, consider what would be suitable for each room. Pale colors and creamy tones create a calm, unified atmosphere. Darker shades are rich and warm, perfect for a cozy, opulent impression.

Color styling

There is no such thing as a bad color, just bad combinations. In a color scheme, one color will feature more than the others. Your first choice is whether this dominant color should be warm or cool.

Warm colors such as red, purple, orange, peach, brick, ocher, and yellow make rooms seem more inviting. They warm up spaces in cold climates, rooms without impressive architectural features, and spatially challenged apartments in urban centers.

Cool colors such as blues, turquoise, aqua, and sage green bring a sense of space, visually pushing the walls back to make the room appear larger.

As a starting point you can choose a color that is already in the room, perhaps in the soft furnishings or in a picture, and find partners for it to create your scheme.

Neutral colors such as cream and beige do not clash with other colors and so create a soft, calm backdrop. In a mainly white room, mix cream walls with white woodwork and trims to introduce a subtle color conversation and add interest to the room.

Define different surfaces by playing with light against dark shades—for example, paint a yellow nook or alcove in a blue wall.

Experiment with accent colors—small areas of total contrast, which add interest to the room. For example, a turquoise room can be magical with a dash of coral, a bit of gold, and a pinch of black. The accent color may be in the form of pillows, a vase, or an item of furniture.

Blue and blue-and-white rooms are generally fresher and more serene than rooms colored in tones from the opposite side of the color wheel.

ABOVE By using cherry red above a pure white section of paneling there could hardly be a greater sense of contrast. The red is continued onto the ceiling, thereby visually lowering it, making the whole dining experience a more cozy affair. White lampshades with red linings echo the rest of the decor.

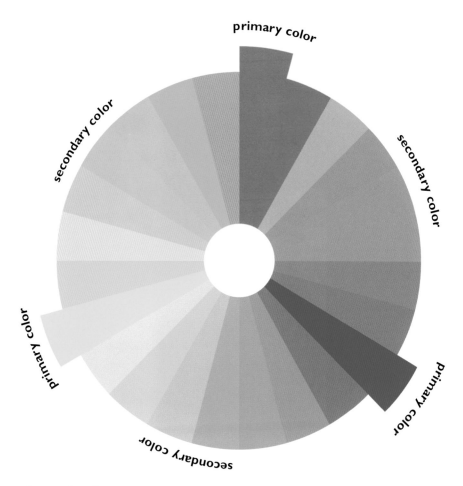

primary color

secondary color

secondary color

primary color

primary color

secondary color

▶ If your room is small, use the same color on all walls. In larger rooms, try using different tones of the same color.

▶ Ceilings will appear higher if you paint them pale shell pink or creamy white. Glossy lacquered finishes also add to the illusion of height.

▶ If you love white walls, choose paint with a good chalky matte finish and then tint it with a little something extra for a hint of depth and sophistication.

Color wheel

A color wheel is an illustration of the colors of the rainbow, rearranged into a circle. It shows color families, and how colors can be mixed to make any hue, apart from black and white. It also helps identify harmonizing and contrasting colors.

Primary colors are red, yellow, and blue, the only colors that can't be made from other colors.

Secondary colors are made with equal amounts of adjacent primary colors, creating orange (red and yellow), purple (red and blue), and green (yellow and blue).

The blue side of the wheel has cool colors, frequently used for washing areas.

The orange side of the wheel has warm colors and so are most often used in living rooms and bedrooms.

Contrast colors are on opposite sides of the wheel, such as green and red, and are often used together with one shade dominating and the other used as an accent color.

Harmonizing colors are close to each other on the wheel, such as yellow and orange.

ABOVE The dominating color in this living room is blue, used in different tones on the walls and behind the shelves used for storage and display. Splashes of bright yellow add interest to the scheme.

Types of paint

There is a huge variety of paint types available, and it is worth considering your choice carefully if you want a finish that will look good for years, not months.

For walls and ceilings

For these surfaces waterbased paints offer good coverage and are easy to clean from rollers and brushes.
Latex paint dries quickly and is the best choice for covering large surfaces.
Matte latex leaves a dull, flat finish. A textured version is thicker, and is good for covering poor surfaces.
Vinyl matte latex is harder wearing than plain matte.
Vinyl silk latex is hardwearing with a high-sheen finish.
Eggshell is oil based, with a medium sheen. There are quick-drying, water-based acrylic equivalents.

For wood and metal

Paint for wood and metal was once made with lead. This was replaced by oil, which is still used but is now slowly losing out to water-based paints, which are easier to use and kinder to the environment. Both these surfaces need a coat of primer paint the first time they are painted.
Primer seals and stabilizes untreated surfaces that are being painted for the first time.
Gloss is usually oil based but water bases are increasingly popular. Gloss provides a shiny, hardwearing finish, making it first choice for heavily trafficked areas.
Eggshell is good for poor surfaces and produces a medium sheen. Two coats are usually needed.
Varnish is a resin solution used to coat and seal bare wood, giving it a glossy, transparent finish.
Wood stain is an oil-based coating, which leaves a hardwearing natural or colored finish that shows the grain of the wood.

ABOVE Colorwashes create a distressed look in this bathroom with its Mediterranean terra-cotta walls and pale blue ceiling.

RIGHT A floral stenciled pattern in deep purple stands out from the lilac wall. Note the harmonizing colors of the accessories.

 ## PROFESSIONAL ADVICE: DECORATIVE TECHNIQUES

Painted walls don't have to be plain. There are many techniques, such as those below, for adding interest to the finish. You might be able to apply these straight to your existing walls if the color and surface quality is good enough. If possible, test out the technique on paper first—often the trick is to minimize how much paint is being applied. Use latex paint or glazes, which are a blend of mineral spirits, linseed oil, and oil or acrylic paint.

Bagging: Use a plastic shopping bag (the kind in which groceries are packed) to apply paint that results in a mottled appearance.

Checks: Turn stripes (see below) into checks by painting horizontal stripes of a different color over existing vertical ones.

Ragging: Dab a scrunched-up paint-dampened rag on the wall to create a patterned effect, turning the rag so the pattern is random. Twisting the rag, soaking it in paint then squeezing it almost dry and rolling it gently down the wall is called rag rolling.

Sponging: Dip a naturally textured damp sea sponge into the paint or glaze and remove the excess before applying. For a dappled effect, rotate your hand as you work.

Stamping: Buy or make stamps to print friezes or allover patterns on the wall.

Stenciling: Stencil brushes are best for dabbing paint through a stencil, but you could also use a natural sea sponge, stenciling crayons, or spray paints (always use a mask).

Stippling: Use a glaze and stippling brush and work in sections, applying the colored glaze as evenly as possible, dabbing the brush lightly on the wet glaze after you apply it. Do not overlap stipples and work from left to right and top to bottom.

Stripes: Use latex paint and specially designed rollers, or try white gloss on white latex for a subtle effect. Mark out stripes with chalk or masking tape, or paint the stripes freehand using your roller.

ABOVE Pale blue stencils in a regular pattern show through subtly against the aqua walls, which echo the color of the table.

LEFT Freehand painting in diluted white latex paint with a partly sponged ceiling creates a distinctive look in this living room.

Set ...

Now that you have selected your colors and have decided the type of paint you would like to use—and how you are going to apply it—it is time to get your room ready for its overhaul.

Preparation and planning

Whether you are planning on doing the painting yourself or getting someone in to do it, thorough preparation is the key. Expect to spend twice as much time on preparation as on painting, that way you won't have to repeat the job the following year.

Protect your furniture and floors. If it isn't possible to move all the furniture out of the room, at least stack it in one area and cover it with dropcloths or protective sheets. Cover the floors, too.

If there are rugs or carpets in the room, roll them up fully, or at least 2 feet in from the wall—paint has a habit of splattering. Tape plastic bags over fittings such as wall lights (remove the bulb first) and door knobs.

Check on the state of your walls. Small holes and cracks need to be filled in with a spackling compound before painting and then sanded down thoroughly once dried. When filling, mix a little paint into the compound to avoid pale patches.

Sand and seal the walls. If you have a large area to be prepared, consider renting an electric sander for the day. Dusty walls and new plaster would also benefit from being sealed with diluted polyvinyl adhesive before being painted. Wear a mask when sanding. Wipe dust from sanded walls.

Calculate how much paint you need. Measure the total surface area. On average, one gallon of paint covers 87 square yards, although vinyl silk latex doesn't stretch quite so far. Buy all the paint you need at the same time, as colors can vary between batches.

Mix the paint thoroughly. This is always necessary to ensure that paint components are combined and the texture is smooth. Lift the stirrer up and down as well as around and around to make sure the bottom of the paint is as equally well mixed as the top.

If working with bare wood, seal the knots, otherwise you'll have gooey resin showing through in a few months. Then cover the wood with one or two coats of primer paint.

Strip or sand down all wooden surfaces.

Gloss paint needs a primed surface to stick to. Apply an undercoat, and sand it gently when dry. Two coats of gloss (sanding after the first) on top of the undercoat will create a smooth finish.

Always wipe down sanded surfaces to get rid of dust before applying the next coat of paint.

PAINTING EQUIPMENT

Brushes: Come in many shapes and sizes; perfect for cutting in and painting intricate details; use on large areas.

Roller: Ideal for open surfaces; quick and efficient; sizes vary. However, can be too large for cutting in and the texture across a wall can vary.

Sprayer: Good for painting broad wall surfaces; also useful for inaccessible areas such as behind pipes; can be messy, so thorough covering of all surfaces is necessary.

Pads: Suitable for large surfaces; small ones are useful for cutting in; less messy than rollers; ridges can form if paint is not spread evenly between applications.

ABOVE White is so useful as an accent color and here its use on the chair rail, fire surround, ceilings, woodwork, and furnishings unifies the room and contrasts strikingly with the strawberry red walls and chair cover trim.

RIGHT The tree and swan motifs painted here achieve a startling effect that is almost like a trompe l'oeil as it deceives the eye. Geometric patterns on the ceiling are reflected in the flooring.

Decorate!

This is the fun part, because you'll see the room change dramatically as you effect the transformation. Keep the room well ventilated to aid drying and to get rid of nasty odors and gases. Check your feet every time you leave the room, otherwise you might decorate the carpet outside, too.

Order of painting

1 Paint ceilings first.

2 Prime and undercoat wood.

3 Apply two coats of matte on the walls, painting the edges first, then working in horizontal bands.

4 Apply a top coat of gloss paint on wood, painting vertically with the grain.

Ceiling tips

Wear goggles.

Use a platform—it's much better than getting a stiff neck.

Start in a corner near a window.

Paint the edges first (use a small brush—it takes longer, but it's worth it—see opposite).

Apply paint with a roller, brush, or pad in 2-foot bands.

Apply each fresh load of paint just clear of the last paintwork, then blend it in.

Keep the edges wet so that fresh paint blends in.

ABOVE Rag rolling in gold and cream over a dusky pink wall creates a sense of airy space, emphasized by the dark scarlet of the lower wall.

RIGHT Painting the ceiling the same bold pink as the wall keeps this large space intimate, and the natural light flowing through the window provides sufficient visual contrast to avoid the effect becoming too sugary. Scattered pillows provide the accent colors.

OPPOSITE A colorwash of sea blue on olive green on the window wall draws the eye across the room. The dark walls contribute to keeping this large room cozy and welcoming, with the warm golden glow of the sofa inviting us in.

PROFESSIONAL ADVICE: THE PERFECT FINISH

Tool organization: Be sure you have all the necessary tools on hand before you begin. Once you are up a ladder with a paint can in your hand, you won't want to go elsewhere for a rag to mop up any drips or accidental spills.

Cleanliness: Rinse out your paintbrush or roller regularly. Paint can clog up these items, resulting in an uneven application of paint.

Use daylight: Paint with an indirect light source. It can be difficult to see where you have painted, especially on second or third coats of paint, so paint in natural daylight as much as possible.

Good technique: Paint well-defined lines at the edges of the walls—professionally known as "cutting in." This is most important where wall meets ceiling and is best done with a 2-inch-wide brush. As you paint along a wall, be sure to keep the edges of the painted area wet as this will avoid shading variations.

Paint management: Don't fill trays and paint buckets too full. For a roller tray, fill to the bottom edge of the ribbed slope only; fill a paint bucket to no more than one-third. Taking a break? Pop your brush or roller in a plastic bag, or wrap it in plastic wrap to stop it getting sticky and drying. Do the same with paint trays or buckets.

Double check: Think you've finished? Leave the room for a few minutes and then come back in to check with a fresh pair of eyes. There are bound to be areas that need a touch more paint, or little gaps that need finishing off.

Painting other surfaces

You'll be using gloss paint on wood and metal surfaces like doors, windows, and radiators. Oil-based paint is less forgiving than water-based paint, so follow these tips:

Wipe surfaces first with a tack cloth, or damp with mineral spirits. Dust grains that show up under paint are impossible to get rid of.

Keep a cloth soaked in mineral spirits handy. Use it to wipe off mistakes and to keep your hands clean.

Don't apply oil-based paint too thickly, it will run. You'll get the best finish from two thin coats, the first lightly sanded down before the second coat is applied. You can thin down gloss paint with 10 percent mineral spirits.

Try to paint in the direction of the grain. Most of the time, your strokes should be vertical.

Start by painting a thin strip around all edges, then cover larger areas with a wider brush or roller.

When finished, brush as much paint as you can onto newspaper before cleaning the brush in mineral spirits.

If you have any accidental spills, wipe up immediately or let dry and scrape off with a spackling knife.

Remove dry paint from a carpet by scraping the paint with a craft knife held at an angle to the floor (to avoid damaging the pile). You can then vacuum up the flakes and your carpet should be like new.

Painting windows

To mask or not to mask? Sticking masking tape along window edges will stop paint from getting on the glass, but you'll still have to clean off the adhesive. To save time and effort, use painter's tape instead, or leave the window as it is and scrape off any stray paint later.

Scrape within a couple of hours of painting if you can: the paint won't have completely dried on.

Paint the inner edges first.

Apply paint as thinly as possible on any runners and edges that meet, so that the window will still close well.

Don't paint sash cords.

Try not to paint windows in direct sunlight. The paint could blister in the heat, and the glare will make the job hard work for your eyes.

STORING MATERIALS AND EQUIPMENT

Don't hammer lids down (they will buckle). Instead, put a piece of wood across the lid and tap it down. Shake the can to form an air lock.

Label paint cans with the color and the location where it was used. If you need to touch up any areas that get damaged, you'll save hours of head scratching.

If possible, store paint in the house as it doesn't like changes in temperature.

A layer of plastic wrap on top of the paint prevents a skin forming on the paint's surface.

To store brushes, when they are dry hang them from hooks to keep the bristles straight. If you can't do this, wrap them in newspaper to prevent the bristles splaying.

Dry metal items such as paint trays thoroughly to prevent them from rusting.

Wash the drop cloths so they will be ready to use next time.

ABOVE Neutral colors in the cream sofa and light tan fire surround provide a calm backdrop for the olive green molding and shutters.

LEFT Painting the curtain rod white to match the baseboard balances the effect of the aqua walls and green upholstery.

Inspirations

In small spaces, light colors such as white and neutrals maximize the amount of reflected light, making the room seem larger, as two of these pictures show. Plan your color scheme floor by floor, rather than room by room, to achieve continuity throughout the home.

ABOVE Maintain continuity between rooms and across large areas by choosing similar shades of the same color. Here the mustard hall teams beautifully with the sunny yellow of the far room.

LEFT Neutrals can become bland if overused, but here this is avoided with the clever texturing of the walls. Accent colors and visual interest are provided by the intriguing accessories such as the Plexiglas chair, orange stools, and the earthy hues of the pillows and pictures.

LEFT Wood paneling and painted bricks provide texture in this setting where the use of white keeps a compact space bright and lively.

ABOVE The mottled white effect on the dusty pink wall creates a timelessly stylish backdrop for the Gothic statues and chandelier.

▶ Position motifs centrally to a wall or space. This is especially important for larger designs.

PAGE 28 FOR PAPERING TIPS

▶ With a wide variety of wallpaper styles to choose from, you can either coordinate with your soft furnishings or go for something entirely different.

PAGE 24 FOR TYPES OF WALLPAPER

▶ In a large room like this, big patterns on wallpaper don't overwhelm, but bear in mind scale when making your choice.

PAGE 25 FOR WHAT STYLE?

▶ Choose your paint colors to complement the wallpaper. Here a dark band of blue runs around the room to reflect the blue rim of the vases in the wallpaper.

PAGES 10–11 FOR PAINT COLORS

WALLPAPER

If you're not going to paint the walls, start choosing the wallpaper. This is a fast route to altering the character of a room, and with the right preparation, can be a joy to complete yourself.

Ready?

Wallpaper changes the look of a room both quickly and dramatically. The wide variety of styles, patterns, and textures available offers a multitude of design choices—indeed, selecting the wallpaper is the trickiest part of the whole process. Hanging it is a fairly straightforward job that an amateur can successfully accomplish.

Types of wallpaper

First, choose the best material for the room. Consider such questions as: is it a heavy traffic area, so do the walls get dirty? Is condensation a problem?

Embossed or relief wallpapers have a thick texture and a raised finish that is tough and spongeable. They are good for hiding imperfections in wall surfaces.

Fabric wallcoverings are of finely woven cotton, linen, or silk, which is then backed with paper. They give an elegant finish, but are harder to hang than paper, some of which can replicate the look of fabric very well. Tougher fabrics such as burlap are unbacked. They are used to add texture, hide imperfections, and can be wrapped around panels, which will be attached to the wall.

Flocked wallcoverings have a relief pattern created by gluing fiber onto paper, creating a raised velvet-like texture. The effect can be warm and sumptuous.

Lining paper is smooth, off-white paper that forms a good base for paint or wallpapering. Badly cracked or blemished surfaces benefit from this material.

Printed (or decorated) paper carries a printed motif or pattern and is available in a range of designs, colors, qualities, and cost. The priciest, hand-printed paper, is tricky to hang because matching the patterns is difficult.

Vinyl-coated wallpaper is flat, decorative paper that is covered in a thin layer of clear protective vinyl, which can be embossed. It has the great benefit of being

ABOVE Textured wallpapers that resemble grasscloth or other similar natural fabrics introduce variety to a neutral decor.

RIGHT This intricately and elegantly patterned wallpaper draws the eye but does not dominate the landing space due to its light coloring.

WALLPAPER

▶ Choose your wallpaper before the paint—it's easier to find a match that way.

▶ Get the largest samples that you can, so you can really see the effect. Sometimes color balances work differently on a larger scale, and what looked great as a small sample disappoints once it is covering a whole wall.

▶ Study samples in natural light as well as in the rooms where they'll be used.

▶ Buy an extra roll of paper for future repairs.

washable, making it suitable for bathrooms, kitchens, and children's rooms.

Woodchip is a very cheap, rough-textured paper suitable for concealing the poor condition of a wall. It is more difficult to cut or remove than other wallpapers.

What style?

Large patterns reduce the size of a room, bringing the walls in toward the viewer.

Small patterns on a pale background give the impression of space, as long as the pattern is not too dense.

Vertical stripes make a room look taller.

If there is a dado rail, molding, or other horizontal dividing line, using different papers on each side of it adds to the feeling of height.

Bold, geometric designs suggest order and formality.

Borders provide a formal finish, framing an area or serving as a dado rail. They can also work well at other levels such as those of baseboards or chair rails.

To unify a room with a sloping ceiling, such as a bedroom that nestles under the eaves, continue the wallpaper onto the ceiling.

ABOVE If this room were any smaller, the large pattern of the matching wallpaper and seat covers would overwhelm the space.

LEFT Narrow stripes make the wall seem taller, and their closeness creates interesting visual texture behind the simple framed prints.

Set ...

Hanging wallpaper is not a job to do in a hurry, but if you are well organized, it can be done neatly and efficiently. You don't want to get the paper dirty, so wear rubber gloves and have a clean sponge handy. Complete all painting work in the room (including the ceiling) before you start hanging the wallpaper—paintwork is more forgiving of drips than wallpaper is! If there is old wallpaper on the wall, it must be removed and then the surface prepared.

Removing old wallpaper and preparation

If the room is large, or you are doing more than one room, hire a steam stripper and follow the manufacturer's instructions.

If it's a smaller job, pull as much paper off the wall as you can, then let water be your work partner. Apply hot water mixed with a little vinegar (to attack the paste if there's a lot of it) with a brush or sponge in sections. You will already have put down drop cloths to protect the floor, but it is worth placing rolled up newspaper at the base of the wall to soak up the drips first. The water quickly penetrates the paper, allowing you to scrape it off.

Treat obstinate patches by scoring the area in a criss-cross pattern with the corner of a paint scraper or putty knife before applying more water. Vinyl-coated wallpaper will usually peel off, leaving the paper backing behind, which is fine as long as the finish is even.

Wallpaper paste will need a key to grip to, so sand the wall if it has a smooth finish (like gloss paint). If the surface is dusty, seal it with a coat of five parts water to one part water-based glue.

Get rid of anything sticking out of the wall, like nails and screws. If these are for holding pictures etc., mark the spot with a toothpick or matchstick. Only mark picture hook locations if you are sure you will want to rehang pictures in exactly the same place.

If shelves can be removed, do so marking the screw holes.

Mask stains that resulted from dampness. If the surface is dark and your wallpaper is light, give the stain a quick coat of white latex paint.

HOW MUCH PAPER?

Measure the height and width of the walls to be papered, including the windows and doors (to allow for waste). It is useful to know the total length and the square footage you need to cover, as roll sizes vary. Use the manufacturer's guidelines to see how many rolls you need—and bear in mind that they are often sold in "bolts" of two. If your paper is patterned, order extra to allow for matching the pattern on the wall: measure the depth of the pattern repeat, and add this to your figure for room height. If you are papering a ceiling, measure the floor to get the dimensions.

LEFT The marbled effect off the walls echoes the material of the fireplace below. Many wallpapers are available that effectively re-create paint techniques, such as the rag rolled finish here.

ABOVE Small patterns can get lost in a big room, but here the grand sweeping motifs of the wallpaper become the major decorative feature, echoing the curvy designs of the furniture.

WALLPAPERING EQUIPMENT

For preparation: Steam stripper, scraper, filling knife, plumb bob and line or spirit level

For hanging: Pasting table, bucket (with handle) for size and paste, wallpaper tray (if using prepasted paper), pasting brush, paper-hanging brush, two chairs and a broom handle, large-bladed scissors, adhesives (wallpaper paste and rubber), sponge, tape measure, craft knife or small-bladed scissors (for precise cutting)

For finishing off: Seam roller, bucket (different color) for clean water, sponge

To wear: Rubber gloves, goggles (if using a paint stripper)

DECORATOR'S TIPS

▶ You don't have to use a pasting table: you can use any table covered with a wipe-clean plastic sheet, taped to the legs.

▶ If the edges of the table are coarse, they can catch the wet paper, so cover them with a couple of layers of painter's or masking tape.

▶ Stop wallpaper from rerolling by tying a piece of string loosely between the legs at one end of the table. Tuck the end of each cut piece of wallpaper under this.

▶ Mark standard measurements along one edge of the table, so that you can make accurate marks on the paper without constantly picking up a tape measure.

Decorate!

Be really clear about how you are going to tackle hanging your carefully chosen wallpaper. Once papering starts to go wrong, you have a sticky mess with a sorry-looking decorator covered in paste and bits of paper. If your paper is prepasted, each length only needs soaking in a water tray. If you need paste, check the type (see box, below). Mix the paste very thoroughly (a piece of wooden dowel is ideal) to get rid of all the lumps—this is vital for successful wallpapering! Tie string across the top of the bucket to rest the brush on.

Where to start papering

Papering the ceiling? Do that first (see page 30).
With the walls, make it easy for yourself by starting with the simplest, most straightforward wall with few obstructions like windows and electrical outlets.
If there isn't a blank wall, start by hanging a length of wallpaper next to a window, close to a corner. Continue in either direction, working away from the light. In that way, you can see what you are doing better.
If your wallpaper has a large motif that needs to be in the center, start above the mantelpiece, or center it between two windows (if they are symmetrical).

DECORATOR'S TIPS

▶ Pastes are usually powder or flakes to be mixed with water.

▶ All-purpose paste works on light- to medium-weight paper, and can stick heavy papers if less liquid is used.

▶ Fungicidal paste prevents mold growing under water-resistant coverings like vinyl and washable paper.

▶ Heavy-duty paste is for heavy papers such as embossed.

▶ Pre-mixed paste is for heavyweight wallcoverings.

▶ Stain-free paste is ideal for light, delicate paper types.

▶ Prepasted paper is soaked before use: check instructions.

ABOVE Broad stripes in subtly contrasting colors allow the wallpaper to emphasize the height of this room and provide a neutral setting for the other patterns in the room. Notice the harmonizing between the rust bedcover and the checks of the shade.

RIGHT The decor creates links all around this large living and dining space. The pattern on the sage green wallpaper matches that of the sofa upholstery so that the eye finds balance and harmony. The walls in the adjacent area are kept white to delineate the space, but the link is retained because of the white-painted arches and ceiling.

PROFESSIONAL ADVICE: CUTTING AND PASTING

Measure and cut: Measure the height of the wall and add 4 inches to each length of paper to be cut. Then cut it.

Mark: Number each length in pencil on the top of the pasting side in order of use. If the paper has a matching pattern, you might have wastage at the end of a roll, but don't throw it away as it might come in useful for making repairs or in awkward places.

Prepare: Position each length of paper, pattern side down, on the table, with the end of the roll at the edge of the table. Weight down the corners to prevent curling. If there is excess length, tuck the paper into the strings at the ends of the table.

Paste: Brush the paste onto the wallpaper from the center to the edges. When you have covered half the length, pull the roll along the table, again lining the end with the table edge, and brush paste on to the remaining paper.

Fold: Fold the paper in 3-foot sections and lay it in accordian folds (which will each be about 1 foot long), taking care not to cause creases. Leave the bottom length a foot longer, and fold up a small section to stick to the paper, thus preventing it from sticking to the wall as you work down from the top.

Hang: Hang lightweight papers and vinyls immediately. Others need to absorb the paste for 10–15 minutes (hang on a broom handle strung between two chairs, which is why numbering the sheets is so useful). Remove the paper from the same end, so you know it has soaked the longest. Soaked paper is more likely to tear, so support it on one arm. For more information, see page 30.

Hanging paper

Few walls are truly straight, but your wallpaper has to be, so find and mark the true vertical. Use a plumb bob and line, or a spirit level, to lightly mark a vertical line on the wall with a pencil. Leaving about a 3-inch overlap at the top, slide the paper (see page 29 for pasting information) in place along the line. Gently smooth the paper onto the wall with the paper-hanging brush, working down and being careful not to stretch the paper (it will have expanded slightly because of the moisture). Run a scissors tip along the ceiling angle to make a crease to cut to size. Now deal with the bottom edge. Brush to push the paper into the angle with the baseboard or floor, then cut along the folded line and brush down.

Continue along the wall, butting each roll of paper tightly to its neighbor. Match patterns carefully before brushing down the paper. Press the joins together with the seam roller and wipe away any excess paste.

Ceilings

Papering a ceiling is a two-person job and should be done before the walls. Make a platform by resting two planks between stepladders—make sure they are secure. Draw a straight line parallel to the wall from where you will start (preferably a window wall). This line should be ½ inch less than the width of a roll. When you paper, the extra width will overlap. Similarly, add 2 inches to each length of paper to create an overhang at each end of the room. Paper as for walls, with a helper holding the folded rolls, using a tube taped to a broom as a support.

Borders

Wallpaper borders must be positioned to avoid switches and other obstacles. Keep the border level (use a spirit level) and only paste and paper one section at a time as border paper dries fast. If the border is framing or turning, miter the corner. Allow one length of the border to run over the other by about 6 inches, then place a piece of cardboard under the overlap. Use a craft knife against a metal ruler to cut diagonally through both layers. Remove the card and the excess paper, and paste down.

LEFT The border paper set between the beams offers the eye something of real interest high up at the end of the room, drawing the wall towards the viewer. This counteracts the receding effect of the yellow walls. The deep blues and oranges in the border paper match the colors of the rug and seating furnishings.

PERFECT FINISHES: SMOOTH WALLPAPER

▶ To avoid damaging delicate or exotic wallcoverings, paste the wall instead, applying a band of paste wider than the roll (to avoid having to paste up to the edge for the next section).

▶ If you end up with a bubble or crease on the papered wall, slit the paper with the blade of a craft knife then paste and flatten. Very small bubbles often disappear as the paper dries.

▶ Don't overbrush, particularly the seams, as you'll be polishing them to a shiny finish.

▶ Do not seam roll embossed papers. It will damage the raised pattern.

▶ When you've hung a few lengths, go back and repaste any edges that have lifted slightly, then smooth down with a damp sponge.

▶ Minor blemishes can be removed with an eraser or a piece of stale white bread.

▶ Use rubber-based glue to paste down obstinate edges of prepasted paper.

▶ Start papering behind a pipe to conceal the seam. Remove pipe brackets and replace while the paper is still wet.

▶ Window recesses can get damp from condensation, and that will lift the paper. To prevent this, run a bead of clear silicone sealant around the edge of the frame before papering.

▶ To repair tears, apply a little poly vinyl adhesive on the surface and ease the paper into place with a damp sponge.

▶ If you run out of paste, use rubber-based glue.

▶ Change cleaning water and rinse out the sponge regularly.

DECORATOR'S TIPS

▶ **Corners:** Trim to overlap the corner by 1 inch, brushing the paper into the angle. Hang the next length with the butt in the corner.

▶ **Light switches:** Turn off electricity until the paste has dried. Hang the paper over the switch box, and cut diagonally from the center to each corner. Cut off the triangles, leaving about ¼ inch, which can then be tucked in under the loosened faceplate.

▶ **Radiators:** Measure where the brackets are, and mark on the paper. Slit the paper up to the top line of the brackets. Paste and feed the paper behind the radiator—long-handled rollers are available.

▶ **Doors and windows:** Lock doors (or put up a warning note on the other side). Paper up to the frame. The outer edge will overhang. Cut a diagonal line toward the top corner of the frame and gently brush in the paper to the side of the frame, creasing the line, then lift and trim along the line. Leave an extra ½ inch to fold down over the frame.

WALLPAPER

Inspirations

Are you going to cover one wall, every wall, or all the surfaces? These pictures illustrate the different effects that can be achieved by these wallpapering choices. Making every surface look the same unifies the look, while going bold on one wall makes a strong statement.

ABOVE A bedroom should be a calm, restful space, and that requires coordination. This is achieved here by the matching drapes and wallpaper, harmonizing with the bed cover and table cover.

ABOVE This is a tricky space to decorate as the angles of the ceiling break up the room. The solution was to paper the walls and ceilings in one gloriously swirling dusty red pattern, its colors reflected in the sofa and cushions. As a result, the room has its own feminine identity, rather than being overlooked as a passageway.

LEFT Papering horizontally is a clever way of broadening the space by drawing the eye along it. The effect is strikingly contemporary, and the pale green of the paper teams perfectly with the colors of the chairs on the rug, whose shades of red match the seat opposite.

ABOVE This is a modern take on traditional paneling, using a giant basketweave to create texture and linear lines. The natural material is then continued by the seagrass carpet. The look is a reminder that making a bold statement along one wall can define the whole room.

▶ Combine different sizes of tile to create interesting designs or to delineate the edge of a tiled surface more clearly.

PAGES 38–39 FOR TILE SHAPES

▶ Use a tile gauge to ensure tiles are well positioned. This is especially important if there is a corner to tile around.

PAGE 41 FOR MARKING OUT

▶ Break up a large area of tiling with an alternative material. Here a slab of marble has been used as a splashback; it could just as easily have been mosaic tiles or a different colorway of the main wall tiles used in this bathroom.

PAGES 36–37 FOR TYPES OF TILE

▶ Finish off with grouting for a completely water-tight surface. Choose a matching or contrasting color.

PAGE 42 FOR GROUTING AND SEALANT

TILING

If your wall is going to have to cope with water and dirt, it needs tiling. But tiles can add a decorative flourish to any room, not just the kitchen or bathroom.

Ready?

Tiles are tough. They wear well, cope with steam and water, and are easily cleaned, so they are a perfect choice for kitchen, bathroom, and shower walls. But tiles have an aesthetic role, too, spreading color and pattern throughout the home.

The tiles you choose will be on the wall for many years, outlasting the rest of the decor, so selecting wisely is essential. Plain, neutral colors are easier to incorporate into the overall look of a room. If you opt for strong colors, keep the rest of the room toned down. The fact that tiles are breakable and require careful application can put people off doing the job themselves, but it is actually quite a straightforward task, and mistakes can be corrected. So be brave and get that tile cutter working!

Types of tile

The standard tile size is 4–6 inches square, but this can vary, especially with handmade tiles. The main types of tile are as follows.

Ceramic: This is the most common variety, usually glazed for a shinier, hardwearing finish, but also available in matte (which may require sealing).

ABOVE Multicolored mosaic tiling creates a busy, stimulating look for this fire surround recess. The colors have been chosen to complement the deep wood of the dining furniture and contrast with the simple white background of the rest of the room.

RIGHT This brick bond pattern creates texture and visual interest in a small bathroom that really needs white tiles for light reflection.

OPPOSITE ABOVE Plain white tiling is the classic look in many bathrooms and, as here, kitchens, where it helps to make the most of the space in a fairly small room. With its crisp and clinical finish, the end result is one of efficiency and cleanliness.

OPPOSITE Tiling can define an area just as well as paint. Here the white tiles delineate the working areas, while also acting as a backsplash. The saucepans hanging from a storage rod lower the ceiling height.

Mirror: Great for making a room seem bigger, or to be used as a focal point. They need to be fitted flush, with no gaps.

Mosaic: Also known as chips, these are grids of small hard tiles on sheets of netting or removable paper. Mosaic tiles are made of ceramic or opaque glass. They can be used to create blocks of small square tiles, set in strips to create a border, or broken off and used individually to create your own design, perhaps paired with broken tiles. This is a time-consuming, but very satisfying, way of decorating—especially if you have a clear image of what you want to make. Plot it on graph paper first. Mosaic tiles suit curved surfaces, too.

Natural materials: Marble tiles are extremely hardwearing and create a luxurious, rich surface (and they have a price tag to match). Other natural tile materials include cork and unglazed terra-cotta (quarry tiles). Both are good for adding texture and tone. Cork improves sound insulation, and makes a handy bulletin board, perhaps in a kitchen or a child's bedroom. The finishes are also good for flooring.

DECORATOR'S TIPS

▶ If the effect of neutral colors would be too bland, use themed picture tiles to add interest, but be careful not to overdo the design by adding too many.

▶ Tiles in bold colors make a strong statement, especially when they are used to create patterns. Consider painting some of the furniture to match.

▶ If you want to use patterns, tiles are extremely flexible because they can be angled (into diamonds) and cut or mixed to include borders and insets.

▶ Consider the effect of light on the tiles, too—it bounces off the shiny protective glaze. Matte finishes create a less reflective surface.

▶ White tiles are the classic choice for bathrooms, giving a timeless finish, but it can look rather clinical. Enliven with colored grouting, decorative inserts, or a contrasting border.

Tile shapes

Shape is as important as color when choosing tiles. Most are square, but you can use sets or combinations of rectangles, hexagons, diamonds, triangles, or other shapes. Plot the pattern on graph paper first.

A standard grid is the norm, but other options include the checkerboard, using contrasting colors; diamonds; or brick bond (Victorian style) in which the vertical lines are broken up.

Do you want to draw the eye toward the middle, or out to the edges? This will determine whether you use different colors or raised relief tiles in the body of the pattern, or accentuate edges with border tiles or slips (very narrow tiles for defining borders).

Picture tiles are another way of drawing the eye, either single tiles inserted at random, or in sets to make more complex representations. Choose a theme that reflects your own interests.

Relief tiles literally add another dimension, as the image is slightly raised, creating texture and visual interest.

PERFECT FINISHES: ADDING LIFE TO OLD TILES

▶ Consider painting the surface of your old tiles with stamps or stencils using specialist tile paint. You could get a highly individual look for very little cost.

▶ Another option is to stick on decorative tile transfers.

▶ The cheerful brightness of glazed tiles can be enhanced when used as a backdrop for flotsam and jetsam like pieces of driftwood, seashells, or sea glass.

▶ A few antique tiles, or souvenir tiles bought on vacation, can be set among standard tiles to create a personalized wall.

ABOVE RIGHT Here a deep tile border at the level of a chair rail creates a striking effect in this small bathroom. The diagonal pattern brings energy and the bold green is in vivid contrast to the white tiles. A checkered border strip above is continued in the sink recess.

FAR RIGHT Filling the whole space between countertop and cupboards gives a sense of solidity and unity in this kitchen. The combination of a floral pattern on multicolored pastel shades prevents the tiles from becoming too overpowering and dominating the room.

PROFESSIONAL ADVICE: GETTING A GOOD PRICE

Shop around: The prices vary widely. Visit a few tile stores to look at all the layout options. Arrange to borrow or buy a few samples to see how they look in the room.

Picture tiles: Decide how many you need: they cost more than plain tiles but you may be able to cut your order of plain tiles.

Measuring: Measure section by section to calculate the total area (length × width): tiles are sold by the square yard. Then work out how many of your chosen tiles fit a square yard, allowing spaces for grouting. Measure border tiles by length, not area.

Ordering: You are often encouraged to order 5–10 percent extra to allow for breakage and waste. If a professional is going to fit the tiles, or if the area to be tiled is not a complicated shape, go for the lower amount. If your wall has tricky shapes requiring more tile cutting, allow for the higher figure, especially if you are doing the job yourself.

Set ...

Tiling a wall is a much simpler job than laying floor tiles, but, as always, preparation is vital. Smooth out bumps and uneven patches: tiles show them up big time. However, you don't want a perfectly smooth surface. Any minor surface blemishes will be hidden by the tiles.

Preparation

Fill holes and cracks in bare walls. If it is quite damaged or uneven, it may need a fresh skim of plaster. Deal with any causes of damage such as dampness at this stage.

If the wall is painted, the surface needs to be roughened with coarse sandpaper. Strip off any flaking paint with a scraper.

Wallpaper must be removed. Peel off the vinyl kind, and score and soak other types so they can be scraped off (see page 26). Then treat as a bare wall and sandpaper it.

You can adhere new tiles on top of old, outdated ones, as long as they are secure. Wash them down with a household cleaner-degreaser, and sand to roughen the surface. Set the new tiles across the edges of the old set to avoid deep lines of grouting. The outer edges will need to be hidden by wooden battens (narrow strips of wood).

If a double layer of tiles would be too thick, you can pry off the old ones with a hammer and chisel, and then treat as a bare wall.

In all cases, wash the wall to remove dirt and grease and let it dry before applying the tile adhesive.

Obstacles such as pipes are tricky to tile around. You might want to consider having them boxed in.

RIGHT Combining tiles of different shapes and patterns allows you to maintain aesthetic interest. Here the border at sink level draws the eye up from the clean lines of the brick-shape tiles below.

OPPOSITE A zesty green is perfect for the tiling in this compact kitchen. The citrus-green brings a spark of life to the otherwise (necessarily) neutral room.

TILING EQUIPMENT

For positioning: Try square, length of batten, tiling gauge, ruler/tape measure, spirit level.

For cutting: Tile cutter—this is a key piece of equipment. Go for a quality model that leaves clean edges; scorer, score-and-snap pliers, tile nipper (for small adjustments), tile file, tile saw or wet saw (for curves), goggles, grease pencil (for marking tiles).

For tiling: Adhesive, pointing trowel, notched spreader, spacers (or matchsticks).

For finishing: Grout, sponge, squeegee (for spreading grouting), piece of dowel (for molding grout), silicone sealant, and dispenser.

Tiling on a budget or doing a small project? Don't buy, but rent tools such as the tile cutter and wet saw.

TILING

MARKING OUT

First make your tile gauge: set out a row of tiles, leaving spaces for grouting (usually ⅛ inch). Then mark the edges of each tile onto a length of wood batten so it becomes a gauge.

Find the center point of the area to be tiled, and use the tile gauge to decide the horizontal position of the tiles to the left and right of this point. You may need to adjust the center to ensure you will have complete, uncut tiles across the area. Allow, too, for any narrower tiles you have chosen.

Tile from the bottom up. Use a spirit level to check for a level base. If necessary, create a base by nailing a batten horizontally to the wall so its top is the height of a tile (plus grouting) from the bottom. Don't hit the nails all the way in—you will want to remove the batten later! When finished tiling, remove the batten and tile this last row.

Do the easy sections first. If you have to cut at corners, make sure the tiles that meet are matching ones; otherwise the uniform effect will be spoiled.

Decorate!

This is the exciting part. Have a clear plan of where you are going to start, and make sure you have all equipment close by. Keep a damp sponge or cloth on hand when tiling, to keep your hands and the tiles clean.

Applying tiles

If you have more than one box of the same style of tile, take them out and mix them up. This avoids clashes due to variations of shading between batches of tiles. Put aside any faulty tiles; for example, those with cracked glaze. These may be useful for cutting.

Apply the adhesive with a trowel to an area no larger than 1 square yard. Do this as evenly as possible to a depth of ⅛ inch. If you are aware of slight dips in the surface, use extra adhesive there.

Pull a notched spreader at an angle across the adhesive to create ridges.

Press the tiles into place, leaving about ⅛ inch between tiles for the grout; check the alignment regularly. Use plastic spacers or cut matchsticks to keep the gaps even. If you are using mosaic tiles, they can "drift." Reposition with the edge of a spackling knife.

Using grout and sealant

Before grouting, check that you are happy with the job so far and that no tiles are raised higher than the others. If so, pry them out and replace them using less adhesive. Use grout powder, as it is the most durable kind, and use a squeegee to get the grout into the gaps between tiles. Wipe away the excess grout before it dries, then mold it with a piece of dowel slightly wider than the gap, to create a neatly grooved finish. For a completely waterproof joint, just wipe to leave the surface flat. Polish the surface with a soft, dry cloth.

Gaps between the tiled area and surfaces such as a bath need to be filled with a silicone sealant.

Make sure the sealant dispensing nozzle is the same diameter as the gap, and then squeeze the sealant in one continuous movement as you move along the gap. Use a wet finger to smooth the sealant.

ABOVE Tiling needn't be the conventional positioning of ceramic squares on a wall, the same principles apply for something a little more unusual, as on this circular mirror surround. Old ceramic tiles have been smashed and glued to a plywood base in a random style before the grouting was applied.

RIGHT These pictorial tiles add a sense of fun and a burst of color to this kitchen. Used on the wall and as a countertop, their light and breezy style will really cheer people up over their breakfast!

PERFECT FINISHES: TILES

▶ Grouting takes about a day to dry, and air bubbles can form during this time. Burst them, and fill the gap with a little grout placed on your finger.

▶ Remove dried grout with a paint scraper. Put a little dishwashing liquid on the blade to avoid scratching the glaze.

▶ Remove dried grout from a carpet using a stuff brush.

▶ Wash all tools, be sure metal parts are completely dry, and then coat with a little oil to stop rust from forming.

▶ If you are drilling holes in tiles, put two pieces of masking tape on the drilling spot first in the shape of a cross. This will stop the drill from slipping and damaging the tile.

DECORATOR'S TIPS

▶ If there is not room for a whole tile, measure the gap. Mark this distance on the tile with the grease pencil.

▶ If you do not have a tile cutter, score the line you want to cut, using enough pressure to get through the glaze in a single stroke. Line up the mark in the jaws of the pliers, and squeeze. The excess tile will snap off.

▶ Whether you have used a cutter or not, tidy and neaten the edges with the tile nipper, then the tile file. This is particularly important when the tiles are at internal and external corners and you need a clean edge.

▶ If you are going to have to cut several tiles to the same size (for example, in a corner), cut them at the same time.

▶ If cutting a series of tiles to go round an obstacle, number each space and its tile so that you know exactly where each one will go.

Inspirations

With so many choices of tiles at your fingertips it can be very difficult deciding what you want to use where. Narrow your choices by first thinking about what size you want and then if you would like patterns or not, and, if so, just how much.

ABOVE If you are tiling a large area, consider using a mixture of plain and patterned tiles for a more interesting finish. Here two different blue and white patterns are interspersed among plain white.

ABOVE A handful of blue mosaic tiles have been mixed in with otherwise neutral tones to give the back wall of this shower unit the perfect watery finish.

ABOVE If it's a plain white backsplash you are after but would prefer to see the design broken up a little, choose rectangular tiles and lay them in a brick bond pattern.

LEFT These small square tiles make the perfect linear backdrop for the equally geometric shelves and cupboards in front of them.

RIGHT Here, the marble backsplash behind the stove has been given a focal point with the use of mosaic tiles. The colors echo those of the marble with an added hint of lilac for tonal interest.

► In a bedroom, it obviously pays to have comfort underfoot. If you aren't blessed with lovely floorboards, look for wall-to-wall carpets with a good quality underlay or else a large, thick rug.

PAGES 54-55 FOR SOFT FLOORING

► Different rooms have different requirements—see the room-by-room breakdown for suggestions.

PAGE 48 FOR ROOM-BY-ROOM CHECKLIST

► A bare floor can be hard under the feet, especially in a bedroom, so choose a rug to warm things up a little.

PAGE 55 FOR RUGS AND MATS

► With floorboards like this, nothing else will do other than a high-sheen varnish or wax.

PAGE 51 FOR WAYS WITH WOOD

FLOORING

Flooring can't be an afterthought: it has
to be right at the top of the list when
you are changing a decorative scheme.
Get it right, and you have a wonderful
base from which to grow a room that
works well and suits your style.

Ready?

Choosing flooring involves balancing esthetics with practicality. Floors are a key element in the look and feel of a room, but also have to cope with a lot of wear, spills, and cleaning. They are also expensive and should outlast many other changes to the room, so you want to get it right the first time.

Consider how much wear the floor will get, whether it is likely to get dirty or wet and need frequent washing, or be water resistant. What are your priorities between comfort, noise levels, and appearance?

There are three kinds of flooring: hard, resilient, and soft. Advice on each begins on page 50.

DECORATOR'S TIPS

Other things to consider when choosing flooring:

▶ Allergies: Some materials can worsen allergies.

▶ Change of use: Is the nursery likely to become an office or vice versa? You won't want to change the floor material soon.

▶ Children: Kids spend lots of time on the floor, and are dirt magnets.

▶ Lifestyle: Do you often move the furniture around, live in clutter, or make lots of mess?

▶ Period of house: Your flooring material should match the house's style.

▶ Pets: These can spoil carpets and natural fibers.

▶ Suspended floors: These won't be able to hold heavier options like ceramic, quarry, terra-cotta, or other stone tiles.

ROOM-BY-ROOM CHECKLIST

Room	Requirement	Possibilities
Bathroom	Waterproof, nonslip	Carpet with water-resistant backing, linoleum, sealed cork, vinyl
Bedroom	Comfortable for bare feet	Carpets, cork, jute or sisal, wood with rugs
Dining area	Accommodate furniture being moved, easy to clean	Stain-resistant carpets, cushioned vinyl, linoleum, natural matting, wood
Kitchen flooring	Cope with wear, water, spills	Most resilient or hard floors, stain-resistant carpet tiles
Living room	Look stylish but cope with lots of feet	Most floor types, so go for one that reflects your decor
Playroom	Soft and warm, easy to clean	Carpet tiles, cork, rubber, cushioned vinyl
Stairs	Hardwearing, safe, quiet	Long-wearing carpets, natural matting
Summer room	Easy to clean, noise reducing	Brick, ceramic, or quarry tiles, natural fiber matting, rubber, vinyl

RIGHT Wood is inherently beautiful, and this space hardly needs decorative highlights other than its magnificent floor, where the patterns of the grain draw the eye around the room.

Hard flooring

As its name suggests, hard flooring is great for the heavily trafficked areas of your home. It is easy to maintain and very forgiving of dirt. This long-lasting material will age with your house. Available in a huge variety of materials and finishes, hard floors should be laid only by a professional. The exception is mosaic tiles, which, like other tiles previously mentioned, can be put into a variety of patterns with some advance planning.

Your choices

Brick: Floor bricks, or paviors, have a warm, rustic feel and come in a range of colors, mostly warm, natural tones of red, brown, and yellow. Very hardwearing, they are particularly suitable for linking exterior with interior.

Ceramic tiles: Like their wall tile relations (see pages 36–45), these come in a wide variety of colors, decorative styles, and shapes, but are far more robust—so much so, that anything breakable dropped on them is likely to shatter into a thousand pieces (not necessarily good news in the kitchen). Ceramic floor tiles are easy to clean, but cold and noisy underfoot. Unglazed versions are less slippery than shiny ones.

Granite flagstones: An especially hard rock that is less dramatically colored than marble, granite comes in neutral shades of gray, gradually wearing to a soft sheen.

Limestone tiles: These sandy-colored tiles are porous, so they must be sealed when laid.

Marble tiles: These stone tiles are available in a range of beautiful, natural colors to create a cool, elegant, and formal effect. They come in slab and mosaic form.

Mosaic tiles: These small ceramic, marble, or glass tiles are made in irregular shapes and are great for creating patterns and images.

Quarry and terra-cotta tiles: Hardwearing and washable, these fired clay tiles are good for kitchens and utility rooms. They come in natural shades of earth red, which lends a rustic, Mediterranean look, and are available in many shapes, making them very suitable for creating geometric patterns. Quarry tiles are harder, colder, and more regular than the terra-cotta variety.

Slate: Slate is tough, cold, and noisy, but slip resistant, and has a variety of finishes. It offers dusty tones of gray, green, and blue.

Wood: Few materials can rival the character, warmth, and durability of wood. It has a huge variety of colors, patterns, and textures. Most wooden floors require a finish to protect them from wear and tear. When considering the layout, you can choose between parallel, diagonal or concentric designs. You also have a wide choice of colors and grains (for more, see page 59).

DIFFERENT WAYS WITH WOOD

Blockwood flooring, such as parquet, consists of rectangular wooden blocks or panels laid tightly butted up against each other, creating a highly decorative patterned effect.

Laminated flooring is planks or sheets made up of thin layers of wood, such as plywood, the top one of which is a real wood. Its acrylic coating protects it from water and scuff marks.

Reclaimed wooden flooring is wooden boards that have already served as a floor elsewhere and are no longer wanted. They are bound to bear the scars of their years of use. You may decide to spruce up your own old wooden floor (see page 59).

Woodstrip flooring is made of random lengths of wood strips, laid parallel to each other in straight rows to give the appearance of floorboards.

ABOVE These limestone flagstones perfectly suit the warm rustic ambience of this dining room.

LEFT Tiles can be cut to many sizes and shapes and these hexagonal terra-cotta tiles certainly add floor-level visual interest.

OPPOSITE ABOVE Being hardwearing and easy to clean, stone floors are particularly practical for entrances and hallways.

OPPOSITE The patina of life over the ages is evident in old or reclaimed wooden floorboards.

Resilient flooring

Resilient flooring is a versatile material that is particularly handy if you have tricky shapes to cover. It usually feels warm underfoot and is hardwearing and washable, so it is a particularly excellent choice for bathrooms and kitchens. Laying a resilient floor is much easier than laying hard flooring, so is something that you might consider doing yourself (see page 58). The tile and sheet sizes are usually quite large so you can cover a sizeable area quickly.

Your choices

Cork: Cork is a natural material that is especially quiet and comfortable underfoot. It must be sealed with a water-resistant finish, which will darken its tone. Alternatively, buy precoated cork tiles. Remnants can be used to make bulletin boards, coasters, nonscratch bottoms for knickknacks, and scratching posts for cats.

Linoleum: Another natural material, linoleum is available in either tiles (which are easy to lay) or sheets (trickier). Linoleum offers a wide range of colors and decorative finishes, including borders. Its slip-resistance and ability to absorb dents and scratches makes it particularly suitable for high-traffic areas that can get wet, such as utility rooms and showers.

Rubber: Rubber's extreme durability and safety features have long made it a favorite for industrial and commercial flooring, but new ranges of colors and textured styles are making it an interesting option for domestic use, too. It feels warm, offers good acoustic insulation, is long lasting, and easy to clean.

Vinyl: Vinyl is one of the cheapest and easiest floor coverings to lay because it is made of flexible plastic. It comes as sheets or tiles, both featuring good noise and water resistance, durability and practicality. Sheet vinyl is available with a plain or cushioned back, making it comfortable to walk on in bare feet. Vinyl tiles are stiff (all plastic, hard to lay), or flexible (soft and easy to work with) and can be printed with many patterns and colors, as well as embossed textures that simulate brick, ceramic, stone, or wood tiling.

ABOVE It is fun to have a quirky, eccentric bathroom, and the linoleum flooring of this one certainly fits the bill. The powerful three-dimensional effect is achieved with geometric shapes, which are echoed in the mirrors around the room.

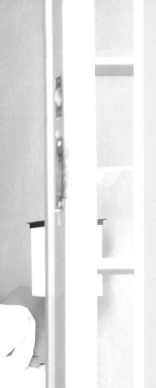

ABOVE For a practical bedroom finish, lay a vinyl or rubber flooring—easy to sweep and clean, resilient floorings are available in any manner of color and pattern. To ensure that stepping out of bed is a more cozy affair, adorn your floor with a rug or two.

PERFECT FINISHES: CARPET TILES

▶ Although carpet tiles are technically soft, they offer similar benefits of flexibility and durability to the resilient materials listed here, and are equally easy to fit.

▶ Most kinds of carpet, including cord, loop, and twist piles, are available as tiles, usually in plain colors or subtly patterned.

▶ Because they are easy to cut, carpet tiles are ideal for novelty designs (perhaps for a child's bedroom) or effects like adding footprints to guide visitors. To make a carpeted footprint path, simply cut left and right foot shapes in a contrasting color, then use the same template to create a hole in the carpet tile, and put the footprint in place.

▶ It is worth buying some spare carpet tiles at the time of ordering, and swapping these every so often with tiles that have been laid. That way you always have a matching replacement tile ready that will have faded at the same rate as those originally laid.

Soft flooring

Soft flooring is the term for flooring materials such as carpets, rugs, and mats, made from wool or other natural fibers. The practical and decorative benefits of wall-to-wall carpeting make it a popular flooring choice. Luxurious, warm, quiet, hardwearing, and competitively priced, carpets come in such a range of colors, patterns, and textures that it's very easy to find one that complements and unifies the decor of a room.

Rugs are another popular choice of soft flooring for similar reasons, with the added benefit of being easy to move to suit the changing needs or roles of a room. When shopping for these products, take a photograph of the room with you to give a true indication of its colors and patterns.

Types of carpet

Once wool was the only choice. Now synthetics offer more options, having lost their initial drawback of being a source of body-jolting static electricity if you had the misfortune to touch something metal in the room. Wool (which hates moisture) and nonabsorbent, colorfast artificial fibers such as nylon or polyester are often combined to make carpets of great durability. The golden rule is, the higher the wool content, the better the quality of carpet, and the higher the price. It is worth considering what type of pile (which means the soft raised surface) you want your carpet to have.

Woven pile carpets have a strong, dense, flattened surface, which is produced by weaving the strands into the foundation.

Tufted pile is not as strong as woven because the strands are attached with an adhesive.

Looped pile has a smooth texture. This can be coarsened if the pile is *twisted*, which results in a much greater resistance to flattening.

Cord pile has very tight loops, so is flatter.

Cut pile has a velvety feel due to the loops being cut. An even shorter cut is called *velvet* pile.

Saxony pile is long, as is *shag* pile, so they wear out more quickly but feel luxurious.

Natural fiber coverings

These provide a useful decorative and hardwearing alternative to wool-based carpets. Available as mats or carpet, they are made of fiber taken from grasses and leaves, spun into yarn, and then woven. They are usually glued to a latex backing. If not, you'll need to attach an underlay. These materials are more rigid than standard carpet, so check with the supplier before buying them to cover stairways.

Coir is a rough, bulky fiber made from coconut husks. It can be natural, dyed, or bleached.

Jute comes from subtropical plant stems, and is soft, so it is not as hardwearing as other natural fibers. It can be dyed and is prone to staining.

Rush matting is made from inland rushes and as they have long fibers, the matting is very long lasting.

PERFECT FINISHES: RUGS AND MATS

▶ The quickest way to change the look of your floor is to add a rug. Traditional-style rugs feature ancient patterns, sometimes in a restricted palette. Modern variations often have more contemporary patterns and a wider, brighter range of colors. They are likely to slip, especially on polished floors, so may need an underlay that grips.

▶ Rugs or mats are also a good way to protect heavily trafficked areas like those near doors and along corridors. Rearrange them occasionally so that they wear evenly.

▶ The different types of rug include:
Afghan: Repeated geometric patterns predominately in bright reds and dark blues.
Chinese: Flowers, birds, and dragons in muted colors.
Dhurries: Flat woven cotton rugs from India, often commissioned for palaces.
Kelims: Wool rugs in bold colors from the Middle East or the Orient.
Native American: Flat-woven to wear as blankets and wraps.
Persian: Lively floral designs, which are woven mainly in rich blues and reds.
Turkish: Striking geometric patterns in soft earth colors.

ABOVE This pale blue and white checked carpet features the two key colors in the room, creating a unifying base while adding textural interest. It also echoes the geometric nature of the striped sofa fabrics and pillow covers.

RIGHT Two neutral shades of cream and soft mustard blend here in the pattern of large squares that leads the eye across the room, complementing the similarly hued furnishings.

Seagrass is made by twisting grass stems, to create a smooth and fairly impermeable fiber that is good for areas that get dirty. Its natural colors (greens and yellows) are spread randomly through the weave. **Sisal** comes from the leaves of a spiky subtropical bush. It is a durable flooring but soft, and can be dyed, bleached, or left natural.

Set ...

The area below your new floor should be clean, dry, and flat. Check with a wooden batten and spirit level. Wooden floors can be leveled with a covering of hardboard panels, but concrete may need a new layer poured over the old one and then leveled with a screed. Some floors "float" on a thin plastic foam underlay. Others are fixed and rigid.

Be prepared

If you will be covering old floorboards, improve dust and noise insulation by making a few simple repairs: fill gaps by hammering in a sliver of wood; screw down any warped boards (better than using nails, which can bounce up); countersink screw holes to maintain a level surface; reduce squeaking and creaks by sprinkling talcum powder into gaps.

Brush thoroughly to remove dust and debris—even the smallest piece of grit will eventually work through and dent materials such as soft vinyl. If laying carpet or sheet vinyl, put down a layer of newspaper to reduce dust.

Flooring materials should be kept in the room they are going to be used in for at least 24 hours to give them time to acclimatize, expanding or contracting according to temperature and moisture levels.

Plan the layout of your tiles or wood panels. Do you want any patterns to run parallel with the wall (focused on a main door or fireplace) or diagonally? Map out intricate designs to scale on a grid first.

Some carpets are made with a foam rubber backing and are ready to be laid, but the better quality ones simply have a burlap backing. The carpet will feel and wear considerably better if it is laid on top of a quality soft underlay, which also provides added protection against drafts and noise.

The best underlay is made from matted fiber felt, because it resists indentations and performs best as sound insulation and draft prevention. Rubber underlays are hardwearing, and are available as solid or (for more springiness) waffle rubber, which comes in different weights, depending on where it will be used.

ABOVE TOP The curves of this gaily colored mat contrast with the straight, geometric lines of the chair above it, while toning with the green floral theme of the wallpaper.

ABOVE Mats offer the opportunity to add texture to a floor, as seen here where the wooden surface alone could seem too clinical.

RIGHT Marble suits cool minimalist decor so well and this spectacular polished floor maintains the flow of light around the room. The dark streaks of its pattern offer a warming touch of contrast.

PROFESSIONAL ADVICE: GETTING THE BEST FINISH

Remove tiles: You will need to remove most types of old tiles before laying new ones—the exceptions are ceramics. Pry them out with a wide-bladed scraper, and remove the old adhesive with warm water or wallpaper stripper. Wear goggles and gloves for this.

Choosing a wood floor: Get the largest samples you can and view them in natural and artificial light before making your selection.

Lift vinyl flooring: Vinyl flooring can usually be lifted easily. To speed up the process, heat the area with a hot-air gun. If the tiles have become brittle, slide a spade beneath to break sections away.

Good edging: A line of quarry tiles makes an excellent substitute for a baseboard; they will match the floor and are easy to clean. There will also be no gap between floor and wall.

Decorate!

Laying resilient and carpet tiles is a fairly straightforward job; just be sure to check the direction of the patterns or the pile before you lay each tile. Ceramic and stone tiles are best left to the professionals.

Laying resilient tiles

You will need: Chalked string, adhesive (optional; many resilient tiles are self-adhesive, while carpet tiles use double-sided tape), notched spreader, craft knife, hammer, damp cloth, mineral spirits, rolling pin, silicone.

Quarter the room to make sure the tiles are set out symmetrically. Lay a chalked string line between the center of two opposing walls. Lay out tiles toward one side to check they fit flush to the edge. If they don't, adjust the center line. Stretch the string at right angles from the center of this line, so you have four quadrants marked, and you can lay tiles from the center point. If the room is irregular, center the first line on the door opening or on a focal point such as a fireplace.

Follow the tile manufacturer's instructions for which adhesive to use or use self-adhesive tiles. Using a notched spreader, spread enough adhesive on the floor to cover an area for about four tiles each time. Wipe off immediately any adhesive that gets on their faces with mineral spirits.

For patterned tiles, work methodically. Start from the center, moving slowly out in each quadrant as you work.

To cut tiles, place the tile to be cut with its edge against the wall. On top of this, place a spare tile exactly over the last tile laid. Draw along the top tile to mark the edge of the tile below, then remove both tiles and cut the marked one to size.

To create templates for tiles cut to fit around obstacles, cut paper or thin cardboard to the size of your tiles.

Make neat pipe holes by sharpening a spare section of piping with a file, then hitting it with a hammer to punch the hole. Cut a slit up to the wall to help fit the tile.

Once you have finished laying the floor, wipe all tiles with a damp cloth, gently roll a rolling pin over them to make sure they are flat, and waterproof the edges with a thin bead of clear silicone.

PERFECT FINISHES: WOODEN FLOORS

▶ Sanding and sealing existing wooden floors gives them new life. Stripped and varnished, bare boards are practical, elegant and full of character. When planning a floor renovation, decide if you want a rustic, distressed look (easier, cheaper, and fine if you'll be covering part of it with rugs) or a highly polished finish (more work involved). For small areas, you will need a chemical stripper. Larger areas require an industrial floor sander.

▶ Damaged sections of floorboards can be removed by cutting through the wood with a tenon saw. Watch out for pipes and cables hidden underneath.

▶ Lift out and turn over any badly pitted or marked boards. When using a crowbar to lift a board, rest it on a piece of wood to avoid damaging the floor.

▶ When varnishing or staining bare wood, paint each board separately to avoid a patchy finish.

▶ The bare wood must be protected from wear and tear by varnishing (very hardwearing) or waxing (which creates a great polished finish but will need regular maintenance).

▶ If the floor is fine but the room lacks a focal point, consider painting a border on the floor to separate parts of the room.

▶ Hand stenciling is another option for adding interest to wooden floors, either as an overall repeated pattern or to create a border.

ABOVE The varying widths and lengths of these old wooden floorboards prevent the floor from seeming too uniform.

LEFT Highly polished floorboards bring an air of formality, while reflecting more light, which is useful in rooms with small windows.

OPPOSITE TOP Checkered tiles are a classic flooring style. Setting them diagonally prevents the corridor appearing too narrow.

OPPOSITE If you like the idea of a checked floor but prefer to use natural materials, consider painting a wooden floor in a checkerboard pattern, as here.

Inspirations

The choice of flooring material should be the starting point for your decorative scheme because it will outlast everything else in the room. However, these pictures also illustrate how the addition of rugs can add warmth, delineate areas, and please the eye.

ABOVE This zebra skin rug clearly defines the area for the desk and chair. It is often a good idea to break up large areas of wooden flooring with rugs as otherwise the overall effect is too uniform.

LEFT This living/dining room with kitchen area at one end really benefits from the way the terra-cotta tiles bring the whole area together, while the linear lines emphasize the proportions of the room. The addition of rugs in the living area brings some warmth and textural variation.

BELOW Natural materials always go well together, as with this natural fiber carpet and the floorboards of the mezzanine.

ABOVE This rug with its bold colors and geometric shapes gives a lift to the otherwise neutral floor.

LEFT Slate has the uncommon ability to appear both warm and cool. Its sleek shininess works with the contemporary setting here, but it also makes the room warm and inviting.

▶ To revive a kitchen, consider painting cupboard doors, replacing their handles, or for something a little more dramatic, replacing the doors altogether.

PAGE 68 FOR CUPBOARD DOORS

▶ Stainless steel appliance doors are less likely to be scratched than a stainless steel countertop, which would benefit from a much more hardwearing material.

PAGE 68 FOR COUNTERTOPS

▶ This combination of countertop and eating area in the middle of the kitchen is a flexible piece of design.

PAGES 64–65 FOR KITCHEN LAYOUT

▶ Spread storage areas around a kitchen so that items like cutlery and table linen can be reached easily and without interfering with chef's progress.

PAGE 65 FOR KITCHEN STORAGE

KITCHENS & BATHROOMS

Kitchen and bathroom style is important because we spend a lot of time in these rooms. The kitchen needs to be a good workspace, but have character too. Bathrooms come with a huge set of practical considerations, but should also be truly relaxing and comfortable.

Ready? Kitchens

The kitchen is the heart of your home. It is where the family eats and socializes, so it needs to work as a food service area and a nice comfortable place to be. The two most important considerations for the design of any kitchen are its layout and storage, both of which require careful planning. Kitchen designers talk about the "work triangle," which refers to the three key places in the kitchen: where the food is kept (the refrigerator); where you prepare and cook; and where you wash up. You need to be able to move easily between these places without having to dodge around a table or hike across the whole room.

Kitchen layout

Have the dishwasher near where dishes can be stacked (by the sink) but also near where china and cutlery are stored (cupboards and drawers).

Remember that refrigerators and stoves are not happy neighbors. Also, bear in mind that cooking often involves carrying and draining pots of hot water, so position the stove near the sink.

You don't need acres of workspace: location is more

DECORATOR'S TIPS

Do you really need a new kitchen? It's amazing how a few fairly simple fixes can transform a tired old kitchen into a room that looks great and works well.

▶ If the basic layout is OK, don't change it.

▶ Paint all the woodwork.

▶ Paint the walls.

▶ Repaint or replace the cupboard doors.

▶ Do the same with old wall tiles—or tile on top of them.

▶ Change accessories such as shades and drapes, light fittings, table linens, and chairpads.

important. The ideal work surface is between the refrigerator and the stove.

It's nice to look up and enjoy the view when washing up, so have the sink under a window.

A central table is great for socializing and as a food preparation space, because you can then face the rest of the room. For the same reason, central islands with sinks, or a warming surface or cooktop and a chopping area, are popular, and take up less space—but they are less flexible in the long term because you can't move them. Map out where everything will go on a scaled grid. Use pieces of cardboard for each item, rather than drawing it: then you can move them around as you wish.

Storage

Once you've got the work triangle sorted out, the next issue is storage. There is a separate section on storage in this book (see pages 104–113), but it is worth pointing out here that you'll need a variety of storage spaces in the form of cupboards, drawers, and shelves. Furthermore, these can be with or without doors, feature dividers or other storage containers, and needn't necessarily be made of the same material as the rest of your kitchen. Look for opportunities to carve storage out of unused space, like above you with a hanging pot rack, or by filling an alcove with shelving.

ABOVE The Shaker-style cupboard doors are complemented by the large and solid wooden table, which is used as a storage unit and worksurface right in the middle of the kitchen.

LEFT Keeping one side of this galley kitchen free of high cupboards avoids it looking too narrow and confined, and allows light to bathe the whole area.

OPPOSITE TOP An island location makes the hob the focal point of the kitchen, and there is plenty of storage space around it as well as above it, which is the ideal location for hanging pots and pans.

OPPOSITE Stainless steel has become a popular material for cupboard doors and drawer facings because it looks clean and stylish. With the added wash of light, this kitchen is contemporary in the extreme.

KITCHENS & BATHROOMS

Ready? Bathrooms

Kitchens are public. Bathrooms are private. This is your chance to create an intimate, comfortable space where you can relax and wash away the cares of the day. There is less to fit into a bathroom, but the space is usually fairly limited, so again, plan the layout, mapping it out on graph paper. Read what this book says elsewhere about flooring, tiling, lighting, and storage.

Bathroom planning

Discuss practicalities with a licensed plumber. He or she should be able to tell you straight away what you can't do and what won't work or would be expensive or too complicated to achieve.

Place the biggest item first, which is, of course, the bathtub. Choose the largest one you can afford that will fit—stretching out in the bath is wonderful therapy. If you have a big bathroom, show off the space by placing the tub right in the middle. That's style! Baths can fit into tricky spaces and make sense of odd-shaped rooms—but make sure you can get in and out easily and can reach the faucets. Allow room for candles, a book, and, of course, the shampoo.

Shower stalls are great space savers and come in a range of sizes. Remember to allow for the condensation they cause, and get expert advice on your water pressure, as you may need an extra pump, otherwise your beautiful showerhead will just dribble on you.

Allow for elbow room on either side of the sink. You don't want to brush up against something or someone while you brush your teeth. Similarly, allow for room in front of the toilet and the bidet, if you're including one. If you choose to box-in the sink, remember to position the sink at the front of the box to prevent back strain and also leave a space of about 4 inches at the bottom of the boxing for your feet.

Toilets are not pleasing to look at, so position them out of the line of sight from the door.

Finally, take an imaginary walk around your bathroom plan: is there privacy where you require it? Are the storage areas easy to reach into? Adjust as necessary.

DECORATOR'S TIPS

▶ Who will use the room and do they bathe or shower?

▶ Which way does the door open? Would rehanging it improve the layout and privacy?

▶ Are all the users of similar height? If not, allow for bigger mirrors.

▶ How is the room heated?

▶ How is it lit?

▶ Is there storage room?

▶ Does it need an outlet for a shaver and hairdryer?

▶ Is there room for a heated towel rack?

▶ Are there special safety requirements like extra handles?

ABOVE While most people still opt for white as the main color in the bathroom, floors, drapes, and shades all offer the chance for some other color interest.

LEFT Sinks need good light, and the installation of a roller blind allows for the natural light to be adjusted easily. Positioning the light over the mirror keeps the light distribution more even at night time.

OPPOSITE TOP If there is space for it, having a chair in the bathroom can seem wonderfully decadent, as you luxuriate after your bath. The towel rail at the end of the bath ensures easy access for drying at the end of a good long soak.

OPPOSITE If you have space, a freestanding bathtub makes a great focus for the bathroom, and somewhere to sit is a real bonus, as here by the sink, with good natural light flowing through the window.

KITCHENS & BATHROOMS

Set ... Kitchens

Once the kitchen is planned, it is very easy to assume you've made all the key decisions and can sit back and wait for it to be installed by your trusted professional. Not so. With major work like kitchen installations, there are many more decisions to be made. Where do you want the power sockets? Where exactly should the lights go? How high should the extractor hood be? If you are not careful, you could be rushed into them without thinking through the answers.

Countertops and cupboards

Food preparation requires surfaces that are very tough, look good, can be cleaned easily, and are heat resistant. There's a range of materials from which to choose: Granite or marble are extremely hardwearing and quite pricey. Because they stay cool they are great as a pastry-making surface, so people sometimes have a small section of one of these materials inset in a cheaper worksurface. Laminates are much less costly than stone and can be produced in a huge variety of finishes, including some excellent representations of natural materials. Check samples to see how they cope with heat and sharp knives. Stainless steel gives a sleek, minimalist look, but scratches and can stain quickly.
Wooden worktops look great but don't cope well with the wet, so you may do better sticking to wooden boards for your chopping surface.
You don't want to get a backache from cooking, so take care that the worktop height suits you. Similarly, set the wall cupboards at a height you can easily reach and also easily reach inside.

Sinks

Get the sink that makes the best use of the space.
No dishwasher? You need a big, deep sink and drainer.
The classic butler's sink is great for traditional-style kitchens. They take up a lot of space, however, and miniature versions are a useful alternative.
A double sink is invaluable for efficient washing up as it allows you to rinse items as you work.

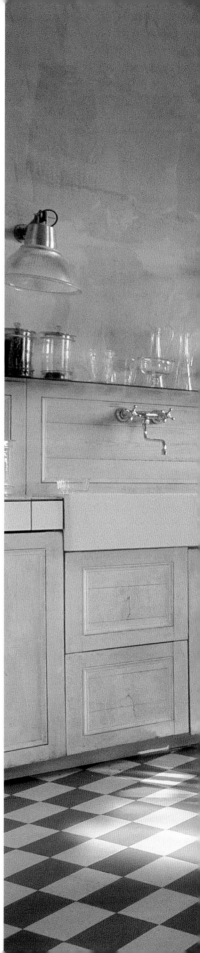

RIGHT Tables make good worktops as well as dining surfaces, and you can easily move them where you choose.

Set ... Bathrooms

You'll need to hire a professional to install your bathroom fixtures, but first there are many decisions to make. Begin by checking that the bathroom floor is waterproof and then see pages 46–61 for advice on choosing flooring. When choosing light fixtures (see pages 114–125), be sure they meet the safety requirements for bathroom use.

Sinks

There are three main types: pedestal (the sink is supported by a stand, which also hides the pipes); wall-hung (mounted on a frame concealed by a false wall); and furniture mounted. The last two vary in style from curvy traditional to sleek modern.

Good sinks have space for the soap as well as a toothbrush holder.

A pair of sinks means no waiting to brush your teeth after breakfast.

If you are tall and need a higher sink, set it into a cupboard top or unit.

Sinks with an integral vanity unit offer excellent storage in a room that often suffers from a shortage of places to put things.

Glass sinks make a strong contemporary statement—but are no fun to clean.

Showers

Again, there's a three-way choice here: over the bath, stall (which stands on a shower tray), and walk-in (the most spacious and luxurious—but you'll need to retile the floor as well as the walls).

You need thermostatic control so that you don't get a freezing blast of cold water when someone elsewhere turns on a tap.

Have the controls put near the door so you can get the water running properly before you step under the showerhead.

Hand-held showerheads are great for washing hair.

Body and steam jets are increasingly available, and wonderfully relaxing.

Bathtubs

Asymmetric bathtubs are designed to be wider at one end, and, therefore, provide more space to sit.

Double-ended baths are perfect for bathing the children together, with no fighting over who doesn't get the taps.

Sunken baths might look glamorous but they are backbreaking to clean.

Half-length baths are perfect for tight spaces, as are corner baths.

Whirlpool baths circulate water through side jets and are becoming more popular.

A bathtub in the middle of the room can look great but it is important to plan the plumbing carefully so that all the pipework is hidden.

PERFECT FINISHES: BATH MATERIALS

▶ Acrylic can be made into almost any shape, and so is usually used for baths for corners and oddly shaped areas.

▶ Cast-iron tubs are strong on style and great at keeping the water warm. Check that the joists can carry the weight of your spectacular cast-iron roll-top bath. If you put the bathtub in the middle of the room, you might also need to raise the floor to allow for pipework.

▶ Pressed steel is lighter (and cheaper) than cast iron, which it can be shaped to simulate.

▶ Stainless steel is a more contemporary option now coming onto the market.

Most house buyers prefer showers to bathtubs.

Toilets and bidets

Be brave: try sitting on a toilet at the store to check if it is a comfortable height.

Cisterns can be hidden behind a false wall or duct. After all, they're not pretty to look at.

ABOVE A corner bathtub is a fine way of making the most of your space. Here it frees up room for an elegant chair.

RIGHT If you have space for it, a shower area with twin basins and a tiled floor allows room for more than one person to wash as splashily as they like at the same time.

Decorate!

Nearly there! Now you can decide on those finishing touches that will refine the style of the room. Go for one eye-catching feature for the "wow" factor.

Faucets

When choosing your kitchen and bathroom faucets, pick them up and weigh them in your hand: the heavier the faucet, the better the quality.

Do you want brass or chrome?

Do you want a pair of faucets, or a single one, perhaps positioned to the side of the sink?

A classic basin faucet with separate hot and cold levers suits any style of bathroom.

Curved pillar faucets complement a Victorian-style bathroom or kitchen.

Neat, thin, single-lever faucets work well in a modern, minimalist room.

Tall spouts suit a contemporary look.

Mirrors

These are essential in a bathroom but choose the frame and style very carefully. Large, ornate mirrors add to a classical, formal look. Intricate frames can be soft and feminine. Lighting around mirrors must be soft and free of glare. Theatrical makeup lights add dramatic sparkle to a large bathroom mirror. Make sure a mirror is mounted at the right height for those who'll use it.

ABOVE This elegantly proportioned faucet has well-designed levers that are easy to use even with wet hands.

RIGHT Large mirrors have obvious practical uses in a bathroom but they are also invaluable if you want to make a small space seem bigger.

OPPOSITE TOP Imaginative design makes even a mundane sink into something that you would be proud to put in a display case.

OPPOSITE A carefully planned combination of curved faucet with a handheld shower head together with fixed shower heads on the wall, make this room the ultimate in versatility.

PROFESSIONAL'S ADVICE:
OUTLETS AND BACKSPLASHES

Electrical outlets: In the kitchen, you can't have too many; arrange them in groups at either end of the worksurface. Outlets should not be located too close to appliances that get hot, like dishwashers and stoves; the heat could melt the fitting.

Kitchen backsplashes: If the kitchen walls are not tiled, you'll need backsplashes behind the stove and sink. These protect the wall from damage and staining by grease, dirt, and water. Glass or metal are both suitable for this role.

Bathroom backsplashes: These are essential behind a sink and around a bath. Usually tiled, see pages 34–45 for advice on choices and fitting.

ABOVE When it comes to choosing the faucets for your kitchen it can be worth spending just a little more money than you might otherwise consider to ensure both style and quality.

Inspirations

The first step in any decorative designing is to look at the features of the room and choose what to accentuate and what to hide. For example, high ceilings are great for ballrooms but rather impersonal in kitchens, so get the lighting low. Small room? Go for a big mirror.

ABOVE It is a great bonus if you are able to have a small informal dining area as part of your kitchen, making the whole room feel relaxed and welcoming.

ABOVE There is evidence of excellent planning here: the high ceiling is left unlit as the lighting is at a lower, more intimate level; the central island serves as a worktop, storage, and serving area; pots and pans are stored practically but esthetically near where they will be used.

LEFT This customer is clearly highly satisfied with the bathroom's space-enhancing mirror with its striking grid of painted wood. No doubt the way in which the aqua-tiled ceiling continues at the top of the wall is also much appreciated.

ABOVE Matching colors on the kitchen area wall and the dining and living room chairs keep the look unified and warm. The wooden floor is also teamed with harmonizing doors, offering respite from the cool stainless-steel surfaces elsewhere.

▶ Soft furnishings are often linked with window treatments. In this room, privacy isn't an issue, so the windows have been left bare. For ideas of window treatments, there is a whole chapter devoted to the subject.

PAGES 88–103 FOR WINDOW TREATMENTS

▶ Adorn pillows with various trimmings to add texture.

PAGES 84–85 FOR ADDING FLAIR

▶ Many fabric designs come in different colorways (collections of prints and patterns in one predominant color); make use of this feature by layering pale shades on dark, or vice versa.

PAGE 78 FOR SOFT FURNISHING COLORS

▶ When choosing fabrics, limit yourself to similar patterns or similar colorways otherwise the effect can be too busy.

PAGES 80–81 FOR FABRIC CHOICES

SOFT FURNISHINGS

Soft furnishings allow you to express yourself creatively and really make your mark on a room. They change how a room looks and feels, both physically and emotionally.

Ready?

Soft furnishings are the upholstery and fabric accessories that add color, texture, and comfort to a room. They are easy to make and are essential to the warmth, character, and style of your decorating scheme (see also window treatments on pages 88–103).

Colors

Decide if you want your soft furnishings to complement or liven up the decor. If you want them to blend in, choose colors similar to what is already there. This may be a little bland, but you could always opt for a change in texture and pattern to add interest. Another option is to choose accent colors to introduce a little sparkle. A mainly pale and cool room is lifted by the presence of inviting cushions in rich, hot tones. A bright and lively room can be calmed by an elegant, cream throw on a chair. Start by looking at your furniture and asking whether soft furnishings could improve it.

Seating

Think about shape and style. Dining room seats have elegant, clean lines, so they need similar coverings such as fitted chair pads with ties. For living room furniture, soft, rounded shapes are more comfortable.
How much wear does the chair or sofa get? The fabric will need to be able to cope with this.
Kitchen chairs have to endure spills and sticky fingers so an easy-care fabric is essential.
Do you want seat cushions tied on or fitted? For example, window seats and cushions must fit exactly.
Revive a sofa or armchair by adding a throw.
Elegant, rounded shapes like that of a chaise longue need soft furnishings that echo them, like a bolster.

RIGHT The harsh lines of this ornate wooden four-poster bed are softened by draping translucent orange fabric above the pink, green, and scarlet striped bolster. The sumptuous colors of both these accessories have been picked out from the carpet, keeping the overall effect unified.

Bed coverings

For a bedcover, do you want an understated look, with the frame visible and the cover tucked in? This is worth doing if the frame makes an attractive feature. Or is it more your style to have the cover hanging informally? If the bed is also used as a seat—which may be the case in a child's room or guest room—scatter it with throws and pillows, with a bolster or two for added comfort. Choose easy-care fabrics for items that need frequent washing like quilt covers.

Table coverings

Decide if you need to protect the table or just want to add decoration.

Large tables can dominate a room so choose a covering that matches the decor so it blends in.

Covering a small occasional table is an opportunity to add color and texture to the room.

Spills are inevitable on dining room and kitchen tables, so your cover fabric must be able to handle frequent washing without losing its shape.

A polished dining table must be protected from heat with a heat-resistant undercloth before being covered with something more glamorous.

If you store things under the table, conceal them with a full-length cloth, coordinated with the rest of the room.

PROFESSIONAL ADVICE: PILLOW TALK

Shapes: Take your pick: seat pads, pillows, and pillow forms are available as squares, rectangles, circles, heart shapes, squabs, and bolsters. Or make your own pillow form and cover if you want something a little more unusual.

Sizes: All manner of sizes are available in whatever shape you require, from the smallest to the chunkiest. Any good home-decorating store or department should have what you want.

Fillings: For a soft, forgiving pillow, choose a natural filling such as feather and down. For allergy sufferers, look for synthetic fillings such as polyester.

For more detail on this subject, see pages 82–83.

Soft furnishing fabrics

There is a wealth of fabrics to choose from for color, pattern, and texture. Don't mix too many different colors and patterns in one room. Below are a number of fabrics that will wear well as upholstery, slip covers, cushions and pillows, and bed and table covers.

Your choices

Brocade: Cotton or a cotton blend with a richly textured woven pattern. It is good for cushion covers.

Burlap: Made from jute or hemp, burlap adds robust texture and can be used for table covers and on walls.

Cambric: Closely woven plain weave or cotton, often used for cushion covers.

Chenille: Tufty velvety cord or yarn with an uneven double-sided pile, which drapes well as a throw.

Chintz: Medium-weight glazed cotton, printed with floral or animal patterns. It is used mainly in living rooms.

Corduroy: Velvet with a regular ridged texture—great for cushions and covers.

Damask: Elaborate patterns in contrasting textures through its complicated silk or linen weave structure. It is used for table linen, cushions, and loose covers.

Gingham: A light, checked cotton or cotton blend that is particularly popular in kitchens.

Hand-woven cotton fabric: An irregular, rough weave suitable for cushion covers and bedspreads.

Linen blend: A heavy, hardwearing linen-and-cotton mix often used for upholstery, but also suitable for tablecloths and cushions.

Madras: Handwoven cotton, dyed, and often patterned.

Moleskin: Great for fitted cushions and loose covers because is it hardwearing cotton that is sensually soft.

Poplin: Light- or medium-weight plain or printed cotton.

Sateen: Cotton with a slight sheen. It is sometimes mixed with a synthetic material.

Sheeting: Usually a cotton/polyester blend made extra wide for use as bed linen.

Ticking: Heavy linen or cotton cloth with narrow stripes.

Velvet: A heavy cotton or cotton mix with a pile cut in one direction. It is often used for cushion covers.

DECORATOR'S TIPS

▶ To choose your fabric, take a piece of white cardboard painted with the main wall color to the store.

▶ Request or buy a swatch of your favorite choices to view them in natural and artificial light in your home.

▶ When making a throw, drape samples over a chair at the store to see how it hangs. You may need a heavier weight.

▶ Check if the fabric is flame retardant. If it isn't, you may want to buy a spray to treat it.

▶ Check on washability. If it isn't preshrunk, allow 10 percent for shrinkage.

PERFECT FINISHES: USING PATTERN

▶ Subtle patterns add a sense of space in small rooms, but can get rather lost in larger areas.

▶ Bold patterns seem intimate and cozy in a large room, but overpowering in a small setting.

▶ Mix bold patterns with plain fabric for a calmer feel.

▶ Floral prints are very traditional in fabric design and are suitable for cushions and small items.

▶ Ethnic prints are more informal and can work well with abstract-style carpets.

ABOVE A table covering hanging gracefully, rather than being primly shaped to fit, lends a touch of informality to this setting.

LEFT Choosing similar colors in different, complementary patterns makes this bedroom stimulating and yet cozy.

OPPOSITE TOP The striped lining visually elongates the canopy, while the fabric on the bedhead matches both the main fabric and the lining.

OPPSOITE Scatter cushions are the perfect vehicle for adding accent color to a room, and they are comfortable to sit on, too!

Set ...

Now that you've chosen your fabric, finalize the style and details of your new soft furnishings to match the decorative look of the room.

Pillow styles

Bolsters offer good back and neck support, and are easy to make. They are more characterful than standard cushions, and can even double up as pillows.

Shaped cushions are a fun addition to a room. How about hearts, circles, or rectangles?

Squab cushions are fitted to the shape of the chair and tied to it with fabric.

Boxed pillows are generally square or rectangular, and it is the cover, which has a wide border all around the edge, that defines the style.

Throws and bedspreads

A throw is a quick and simple way to give a new look to a sofa, chaise longue, or armchair, and also protect against stains. A bedspread or coverlet will do the same for a bed.

Any fabric can be used.

Several throws create a pleasingly luxurious effect.

A textured fabric like chenille and a patterned one like a tartan work well.

DECORATOR'S TIPS

Pillow and cushion fillings should be enclosed in a casing so that the outer cover can be removed and washed when needed.

▶ **Feathers and down** are light and resilient. They are the warmest, softest filling, but some people are allergic to them.

▶ **Foam** comes in sheets, blocks, or chips. It is easy to cut to fit a seat cushion. As it breaks up with age, foam must be encased before a cover is put on. Soften foam shapes with layers of medium-weight polyester batting.

▶ **Kapok** is a vegetable fiber filling used for upholstery. Very soft initially, it gets lumpy, and is not washable.

▶ **Polyester** is washable and nonallergenic. It is sold in bags, or in sheets as batting.

LEFT The bold, bright colors in the picture would dominate without the balancing vivacity of the cushion's similar coloring.

OPPOSITE Details such as these blue and white checked ribbon bows make the smallest item seem special.

Decorate!

Even though there is a huge range of readymade pillow covers, throws, and tablecloths from which to choose, by making your own covers you can add a touch of originality and personal style to your home.

Details matter

This book is not the place for detailed step-by-step guidance, but here are some tips to get you going.

Measure carefully: It is conventional to add a seam allowance of ½ inch to each dimension of the pillow form for the fabric covering. For a closer fit, however, just go by the form's dimensions. In that way it will fit very snugly inside the finished item.

Closures: Although zippers are the most usual closure, you might also want to consider buttons, envelopes (where one side is longer than the other and folds over the top), or ties. For a bolster, gather the ends and secure with a large button (perhaps covered with the same fabric) rather than the more conventional flat finish.

Trimmings: This is the really fun part of making your own soft furnishings. There is an infinite choice in all manner of colors and materials—piping (either ready-made or cover a cord with fabric of your own choice), braids, fringes, ribbons, tassels, buttons, beads, sequins. Just walk around any home-decorating or fabric store and let your imagination run riot.

ABOVE Using a variety of fabrics and styles in one group of pillows produces a series of pleasing contrasts of the colors, shapes, and textures, while remaining balanced as each matches the bedding.

RIGHT If your scatter cushions are in a variety of colors and patterns, a plain, harmonizing background like the green sofa fabric is essential.

OPPOSITE, FAR RIGHT Stripes work well with stripes, as in the different patterns of the chair and sofa fabrics, which team together because the same colors are used in each.

OPPOSITE The geometric design of the center cushion provides a focal point, using colors that are present elsewhere in the room.

🖌 PROFESSIONAL ADVICE: ADDING FLAIR

Buttons and bows: Large, small, fabric covered, plastic, wooden, colorful: add buttons and bows to finished pillow covers and throws as closures or merely as pretty extras.

Contrasting fabrics: Covers needn't be made from one fabric alone. Consider choosing different fabrics for each side of the cover or use a contrast color or pattern for a border or piping cover. For tablecloths, use two contrasting fabrics to create a layered look.

Unusual details: With a bit of creativity, you can introduce some surprising elements to your soft furnishings: appliqué is a great technique for attaching "found" objects, such as fabric leaves or an antique doily. Or consider stitching on one or two clear vinyls and inserting photographs of your loved ones.

Inspirations

As with choosing paints, when selecting soft furnishings remember there is no such thing as a bad color or pattern: just bad combinations. These photographs show how using similar colors or going for contrast can achieve stunningly sophisticated results.

ABOVE The neutral backdrop of the wall and furniture (although the chair trim defines its shape beautifully) allows space for the soft furnishings to shine with their complementary colors and patterns.

LEFT White is probably the only color that benefits from endless repetition, as long as the textures and shapes are varied.

BELOW The cream throw breaks up the robust lines of the sofa, introducing an air of informality with its casual confidence.

ABOVE Soft furnishings can allow you to make the most of the light, as with these dreamily translucent gold bed drapes, exuding sensuality and warmth.

LEFT A group of informally balanced scatter cushions makes this seat inviting and stylish.

▶ An ornate valance is a finishing touch that successfully hides the drape heading and improves the proportions of the window.

PAGES 90–91 FOR INITIAL DECISIONS

▶ Add fringing and other decorative devices to create something truly original.

PAGES 101 FOR LITTLE EXTRAS

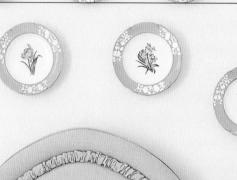

▶ Careful measuring is crucial before buying your fabric; especially if there is a pattern repeat, as here. You don't want to buy too small an amount of frabric, but at the same time you don't want yards of excess.

PAGE 98 FOR MEASURING UP

▶ The length of your drape will be affected by the proportions of the window and room they are hanging in. Full-length drapes have a sense of luxury about them.

PAGE 92 FOR DRAPE LENGTH

WINDOW TREATMENTS

When we enter a room, our eyes are often drawn to the windows, so the way they are presented makes an immediate impact. There is a huge choice of style for drapes and shades, and the fabrics involved are expensive, so take your time to get the results you want.

Ready?

Anybody who likes the look, feel, colors, and textures of textiles will enjoy choosing drapes. They create drama and focus in a room, significantly contributing to its style and mood. They also play an important practical role by controlling the amount of light (and sights) coming in, and of heat passing through the windows. Drapes also soften the hard lines of windows.

Deciding on the basics

Before heading out to shop, give some thought to these main considerations. They will help you determine the finished look you want to achieve.

Color: For drapes, choose a color that matches or is lighter than the tone of the walls, perhaps a hue from your soft furnishings.

Weight: Light materials such as silk or cotton have an airy effect. Heavy fabrics such as brocade lend an elegant, sophisticated look.

Function: Are these curtains mainly decorative? Is insulation important? If you prefer light fabrics, you may need lining or interlining to block out light or to retain warmth. To keep out drafts, have full-length curtains that puddle onto the floor, offering a sumptuous solution.

Heading: How you want the top of the drape to look will affect your fabric choice (see page 92).

ABOVE Doors can be drafty—especially if they are to the outside world—so make full-length drapes to keep your home as cozy as possible. Use tiebacks to keep fabric out of the way by day.

RIGHT The valance for these drapes adds a stylish finish to an otherwise simple heading. The curved and piped edge is a striking contrast to the crisp pleats, rounded off with neat ties along the rod.

OPPOSITE TOP For something a little more feminine, look to fullsome shades or a simple fixed head, as here, with holdbacks.

OPPOSITE If you like to allow as much light as possible into your home and yet still retain a sense of privacy, sheer curtains in white muslin are just the finish you are looking for: stylish and simple.

THE OVERALL EFFECT: How will the drapes fit with the decor in the rest of the room? If you want to attract attention, go for opulent finishes such as swags and tails. If, however, the aim is to blend in, choose a more modern, minimal look using a simple fabric and rods instead of tracks.

DECORATOR'S TIPS

▶ The type of window you are dressing will influence your choice of styles, depending on whether you want to disguise or emphasize its shape:

Bay: The different angles will affect the hanging system possibilities.

Bow: Choose whether to emphasize the curve with tracking or mask it.

Casement: The shapes and styles vary, so choose drapes to suit your window.

Dormer: These don't let in much light, so use narrow drapes or a shade.

French: Need to open wide to allow movement. Use tiebacks or holdbacks.

Picture: Simple designs allow you to choose from a wide range of drape styles.

Sash: Can seem very narrow, so drapes should make them appear wider.

▶ If the window is an attractive feature, don't cover it up, use translucent fabric.

▶ How many windows are in the room, and do you want them all to look the same?

▶ If the window proportions seem wrong, you can change their appearance by adding a pelmet (to add height) or valance (for width).

▶ It is also worth keeping a note of when and how the sun enters the room, as you will want to maximize the amount of natural light that comes in. Privacy may also be an issue here, in which case you might want to combine a panel or shade with your drapes.

Drape lengths and headings

Once you've chosen your fabric, it's time to consider the two most important elements of a drape: the length and style of heading. Begin by deciding the length:

Short: The drape falls just above or just below the sill, necessary if there is a radiator beneath the window.

Medium: The drape falls midway between sill and floor.

Long: The drape falls to the floor, which is good for concealing features like pipes and electrical outlets.

Then move on to the headings, which can be fixed or drawn, depending on whether the drape will ever need to be closed:

Fixed headings: Purely decorative, they create a lush effect, and are very tightly gathered. They require more fabric in the width and tiebacks or holdbacks to secure the bulky material as it hangs. You may also need to combine them with a sheer drape or a shade for privacy.

Drawn headings: Allow the drape to be moved across the window, and can be in simple or ornate styles. The drawing mechanism (track) may be left uncovered (as with a rod) or concealed by a wooden pelmet or fabric valance.

Heading styles

Traditional heading styles often use a heading tape along the back of the curtain, which is drawn up to create the necessary finished effect. The most popular headings are:

Standard gather: The basic kind (also called pencil pleat) has narrow, evenly spaced gathers, which suit pelmets.

French: Also known as pinch pleats, these make a deep, stylish heading good for longer drapes.

Goblet: Uses gathers rather than pleats and is a fuller, softer version of French pleats.

Box: An ornate style often used with valances.

Diamond smock: An attractive, hand-sewn heading using transfer dots.

Puffball: An extra fold of fabric gathers used to create a frothy effect.

A modern heading aims for a light, airy style that complements the look of a room. The drape is hung on rods or tension wires, with no attempt at concealment. Rings are often used from which the drapes are hung, but you could also look at using large ties or use button tabs.

PERFECT FINISHES: LINING DRAPES

▶ Lined drapes look and last better, because the extra weight protects the fabric from fading and condensation.

▶ Lining also improves light blockage and heat conservation—especially if you go for a thermal lining.

▶ Choose a colored lining to make more of a statement; it is an unusual and striking finish.

▶ Use detachable lining if the drape will need frequent washing, or if the lining is needed for extra warmth in the winter months.

▶ Interlining is an extra layer between the main curtain and the lining to add body and insulation—but it also adds weight, which can affect your hanging options.

▶ Fusable web is an alternative to sewing in lining.

ABOVE Covered buttons using the same fabric as used for the piping are an attractive way for finishing button tabs.

RIGHT Full-length drapes allow the light to flood in as they are finished off with stylish rosettes on holdbacks.

Drape hanging systems

Rods, tracks, or wires are the devices you can choose from with which to hang your drapes. All will allow the drape to move, but rods and wires fit the simple, clean look of the modern style, while tracks are more suited to drapes in the showier, traditional style.

Choosing a hanging system

Rods: The basic choice is between wood (fresh-looking, light) and metal (solid, heavy). Pay particular attention to how you want the ends (finials) to look. The rods will need to be attached to the wall with brackets—two for narrow windows, three for most others; otherwise the rod will bend under the weight of the fabric. If you want the rod to match the wall covering, use a wooden rod over which you can glue the wallpaper, adding a matte varnish to protect the surface.

Tracks: Tracks are made of plastic and are screwed to the wall. The drapes are then attached via a system of gliders and hooks, which fit into loops on a heading tape sewn onto the drape. If you want to hide the white plastic track, add a pelmet (which is made of wood, sometimes covered with material) or a valance (fabric). These come in a range of styles and have a major impact on the dressing of the window because they create a visual frame across the top.

Tension wires: These are lengths of wire that are stretched so they won't sag, which then enables them to work in the same way as rods. The wires are good for hanging very lightweight fabrics from clips over a long distance, such as a wide window to create a spare look. They are attached to fittings screwed into the wall.

RIGHT When it comes to hanging drapes, rods are the most versatile of fixtures. When choosing yours, in addition to the material from which it's made, bear in mind the proportion. The larger the drape, the thicker the rod, although, of course, you might choose to make a dramatic statement by incorporating one with a wide diameter above a less than large window. In this room, the brass rod adds contrast color to a space that is predominately decorated in blues.

DECORATOR'S TIPS

Rather than leave a drape hanging straight down, there are many options to tie or hold back the fabric.

▶ Tiebacks: Can be made from almost any fabric, such as cord, jute, ribbon, or rope, and are fastened to hooks screwed to the wall. The hook should be positioned about one-third of the way up the drape.

▶ Holdbacks: Solid fixtures screwed into the wall. They are often sold with rods as coordinated sets, and can be found in wood or a range of metal finishes.

▶ Swags and tails: An extravagant, elegant way of dressing a window, often used in combination with pelmets. They are particularly suitable for tall, wide windows and make an opulent style statement, whether the drape is open or closed. The simplest swag is just material draped over hooks mounted on either side of the top of the window, so the fabric hangs in a flowing "tail." More elaborate swags and tails have layers of fabric and a contrasting trim to accentuate the shape.

Shades

Shades are a practical and simple option for dressing a window. They sit within the window recess (or just outside it) and complement their surroundings, while carrying out the practical job of controlling light and ensuring privacy.

Styles of shades

Plain: These have a flat surface when lowered and draw up to let in the maximum amount of light. Examples include Roman and roller shades. The fabric can be stiffened for roller shades.

Ruched: These are more three-dimensional and opulent, and always leave part of the window obscured as they don't fold away as much as plain shades. These include Austrian and festoon shades. Ruched shades are best made of lightweight fabrics, such as moiré or soft cotton, which gather better than heavier fabrics.

Slatted: When closed, these can fold up as flat as a plain shade, but a simple adjustment opens out the louvers to let in light. Venetian blinds are slatted, but wooden slatted shades are more substantial and less noisy.

ABOVE The simplest of bamboo roller shades means they can be lowered to whatever height you require during the day to keep the glare out and yet let the light in.

RIGHT Rich orange Austrian shades combine with strikingly handsome striped drapes to create a fulsome window display, which is only topped by the dramatic gilded rod.

OPPOSITE TOP For something a little more unusual, these Roman shades have been finished with a black trim along their top edge designed to give a geometric, castellated finish.

OPPOSITE A minimal interior deserves a more restrained approach, as shown here with simple slatted shades with no adornment other than the cords that are used for raising and lowering them.

PERFECT FINISHES: ADDING A LITTLE SOMETHING

▶ Customize a roller-shade kit (these are widely available) with fabric paints and pens to match your decor.

▶ Enliven the main fabric with a contrasting border, whether it's around all the edges or just along the bottom.

▶ Spray old slatted shades with aerosol paint to bring them back to life.

▶ Stencil plain shades with patterns derived from other design elements in the room.

▶ Transform a tired fabric shade with cold-water dye.

▶ Add interest to plain shades with unusual ring-pulls like bows, tassels, beads, or shells.

ABOVE A kitchen is a functional space and so deserves functional window dressings. Roman shades are perfect, especially when made from a simple check pattern: pretty and yet stylish.

Set ...

It is vital to get the measurements for drapes and shades accurate and complete from the beginning. Use an extendable steel tape measure, and double-check each measurement. You don't want to pay for expensive lengths of fabric that will end up in your scrap pile—but, on the other hand, a shortfall would be disastrous. Install the hanging system now, too, to ensure you measure the length of the drapes accurately.

There is not space in this book to take you through making the drapes—it is a long and complex process. If you haven't done it before and want to try, start with a simple, unlined drape. Otherwise, call in the professionals or go for readymade products.

PROFESSIONAL ADVICE: MEASURING UP

GATHERED DRAPES

Width:

▶ Install the rod, track, or wire, which should extend 6 inches beyond each window edge.

▶ Measure its full length, including any return on the track, which will also be covered by fabric when the drapes are hung.

▶ The heading tape you have chosen will be marked with the adjustment needed to make the gathers. This is usually at least two times the rod length.

▶ If you would like the drapes to overlap each other rather than just meet in the middle, add the necessary allowance.

▶ Add 4 inches for each side turning.

▶ Divide this measurement by the fabric width to find how many panels are needed to make the curtains, and round this figure up.

Length:

▶ Finalize the distance of the drop. Traditional drapes hang ½ inch above the floor. If you want the fabric to trail onto the floor, add 2–8 inches. For sill length, aim for ½ inch above the sill, or 2–4 inches below it (this is called apron length). If you intend to tuck the drape behind a radiator, allow 4 inches below its top.

▶ Measure down from the top of the track, or from the bottom of the rings for rods and wires.

▶ Add 8 inches for the top turnings and bottom hem.

▶ Measure the pattern repeat (if necessary) and add this figure to each drop.

▶ Multiply this figure by the number of panels you need. Double-check this figure. Lining measures will be the same, less the pattern repeat allowance.

SHADES

▶ Is the shade going above the molding or in the recess? Fit the batten from where the shade is to hang.

▶ Measure the width. Add 4 inches for side turnings.

▶ Measure the length from the top of the batten. Deduct 2 inches if using a roller shade mechanism. Add 5 inches for the hem.

▶ If the shade will be gathered vertically, add a few inches to allow for ruching.

▶ Divide by the fabric width for the number of drops. Allow extra on this figure for seams.

ABOVE LEFT Shades can either rest within the window's architrave or be fixed in front of it. Either way, it is important to ensure your measurements are accurate. At this window, the plain shades are divided into two: one half you pull down, the other half you raise up.

ABOVE Full-length drapes can either rest just above floor level or puddle attractively—for the best effect, use as soft a fabric as possible. These white cotton sheers diffuse the bright sun so that the bedroom cum office remains pleasantly cool by both day and night.

Decorate!

The last and most satisfying job is hanging your freshly made drapes. Do it properly!

Hanging drapes

Plan to hang the drapes as soon as possible after they are made, to prevent creasing.

▶ Don't do this job on your own: drapes are heavy and bulky so are not safe to be handled alone on a ladder.

▶ Check that the number of hooks on the drape matches the total of runners on the track, including the overlap arm and the screw eyes at the end.

▶ Carrying the drape over your shoulder, not your arm, begin hooking at one end (not the center of the track).

▶ Once both drapes are hung, check where the two sides overlap, and gently adjust so that the pleats are even.

Permanent pleats

This technique will ensure that your drapes hang perfectly in neat folds for years, with the lining, interlining and fabric moving as one. For each drape, you need ten lengths of string, cord, or leftover fabric long enough to tie around the curtain.

Open the drapes. Standing sideways to the window and facing the outside edge, make sure the leading edge of the drape, nearest you, is pointing toward the window.

Start to push the fabric into pleats, by hand, at chest level. As you make each pleat, hold it to your chest. Make sure the outside edge turns toward the window, concealing the lining. If it doesn't, adjust the pleats.

Tie the string around the drape tightly enough to hold the pleats without causing creasing. From a ladder, repeat this process at the top of the drape so that the pleats line up. Repeat at different heights, working down the drape, using the other lengths of string.

If you have the patience, leave the drapes tied up for four days. Your pleats will behave impeccably from then on.

RIGHT Here a cascading valance covers a simple heading on the cream drapes. It also considerably softens the large glass doors and gives respite from the patterned wallpaper and floor.

PROFESSIONAL ADVICE: LITTLE EXTRAS

Bows and bobbles: You can purchase bobbles attached to a tape and sew them to the top of the heading or down the leading edge of a drape (the edge that pulls towards the center) to make attractive additions. The same goes for bows—but they'll need to be stitched on individually.

Tiebacks: These don't have to be made from the same fabric as the drapes themselves. Use them as an opportunity to add some contrast or for a bit of frippery. They may be small but they can shout very loudly if you choose to let them.

Hem weights: These small metal disks add weight to the bottom of a curtain and so if you stitch them into the hem, they help the drape to hang well.

ABOVE Tiebacks can be as simple or frivolous as you like. You can also dress them up or down to suit the occassion. Here, it's Christmas time, so small baubles have been added for a touch of festivity.

Inspirations

Window treatments really are the crowning glory to any room. They can be as simple or as ornate as you wish and with so many fabrics and embellishments to choose from it's a wonder windows ever get dressed at all. Here are some more ideas for you to take into consideration.

ABOVE If privacy isn't a concern, consider a simple "swag and tail" effect to make an otherwise plain window just a little prettier. Team and tone with pillow covers for the complete picture.

LEFT Contrast trimmings around the edge of a shade or drape always adds just that bit more interest—especially valuable if you have chosen a plain fabric for the main body of the shade. Choose something contrasting, as here, or more neutral for a subtler finish.

LEFT Roller shades are the simplest way to dress your window. Here a rich emerald green has been chosen to contrast with the yellow of the paintwork, thereby making more of a statement.

ABOVE Soft cream drapes have been given added interest by the scalloped leading edges, which add shapely interest, and bobbled braid, which gives textural contrast to the whole concoction.

▶ Closets are the perfect solution for possessions that you want to hide away. Fitted out with plenty of shelves, you can then amass items of all manner of sizes and shapes behind the doors.

PAGES 106–107 FOR BASIC DECISIONS

▶ Use shelves for storing books or displaying favorite objects—or both!

PAGE 110 FOR POSITIONING SHELVES

▶ Even logs benefit from a good container to store them in. A rustic woven basket is just perfect.

PAGES 108–109 FOR STORAGE IDEAS

▶ Large boxes make excellent storage containers and can double-up as side tables too.

PAGES 108–109 FOR STORAGE IDEAS

STORAGE

We all amass possessions. Some are things we need all the time, others come in handy occasionally, and still others are there simply because we like them. Choosing where they go affects how smoothly our lives will run, and how much enjoyment they will give us.

Ready?

Storage is often the main cause of frustration people have about their home. The location, rooms, and decor may be great, but if there isn't space for all your stuff, you might feel like you've outgrown your home, and want to move. Storage is partly about your attitude to life. To some people, a cluttered room is cozy and familiar, while to others it looks disorganized and uncared for. They'd prefer the sense of space and freedom that is provided by linear lines and tidy closets.

What are your needs?

Do I use this thing? If you haven't used something in the last year, you either don't need it, or you've kept it for sentimental reasons. Be brave and throw out or give away those objects that you don't use and don't want to look at. There is an old Chinese proverb that says, "Throw away something old and let something new into your life." But if you want to keep something, you should think about displaying it so you can enjoy it. Now move on to what you are keeping.

How often is it used? If you don't use it a lot, it doesn't need to be at hand and can be stored in the attic or a high closet.

With what should it be stored? Store similar items together. Things like games, china, CDs, videos, DVDs, and collections should be kept together for practical and aesthetic reasons. This will also help to clarify your storage needs because different-sized objects will benefit from large- or small-scale settings.

Where should it be stored? This is pretty obvious for kitchenware, but you might be more comfortable keeping sentimental objects in your bedroom rather than, for example, in the hallway.

How should it be stored? There's a rule to follow here: get everything off the floor and onto the walls or behind doors. That gives you three storage options: drawers, closets, and shelves, all of which might hold storage containers—there are many styles of storage boxes available to you, ranging from natural woven wicker to heavy-duty decorated cardboard.

S
T
O
R
A
G
E

PROFESSIONAL ADVICE: WHAT STORES WHAT

Drawers: Great for things you don't need to display and that are hard to store tidily—such as board games, toilet rolls, or saucepans—but that you want easy access to. Buy specially designed dividers so that you can sort out all your belongings, rather than having them filling up the space in an untidy and haphazard way.

Closets or cabinets: These fit the bill for bulkier or smaller items, like clothes, spices, or china. Corner cabinets can make a room layout more interesting, and fitted cabinets can look like part of the wall. Corner closets enable you to store a huge amount of clothes—whether hanging or on shelves—and make good use of areas in a room that might otherwise be wasted.

Shelves: Suitable for items you use a lot or that are attractive to look at and enhance the decor.

Built-in storage: Uses space really efficiently but can lack flexibility and has to be left behind if you go to live elsewhere.

Free-standing storage: Can be put anywhere, including in the van when you move out.

ABOVE If it is attractive, make a feature of it. That is the message from this simple display of cosmetics and matching towels conveniently placed just above a washstand.

LEFT Corner alcoves are ideal locations for shelves as they are perfect for unobtrusive display of collections and curios.

OPPOSITE TOP Displaying a few special objects like these softly curved vases alongside practical items gives a lift to areas of open storage, allowing them an esthetic as well as a functional role.

OPPOSITE Soften the hard contours of doors by replacing them with fabric panels that enhance your decorative scheme and hide the unsightly clutter of things we all need but don't want to display.

Set ...

When it comes to planning your storage, it helps to haved an idea of the storage possibilities that will work well for each room of the house. Here are some ideas.

Living rooms

Cube shelving is ideal for displaying objects without blocking light. A mix of low cupboards with open shelving above offers storage and display opportunities.

Kitchens

Good storage is vital here. Perishable foods need to be kept somewhere cool, dark, and well ventilated—wire baskets stacked in a pantry are ideal. Large drawers at waist or knee height are great for saucepans and small appliances. Wall-mounted racks store plates efficiently, while wall-mounted storage grids are great for hanging frequently used utensils. Cup hooks on the shelves of a hutch offer an attractive alternative to stacking. Overhead hanging racks let you store pots and pans out of the way but within reach.

Halls and stairs

The hall is the first and last thing you see as you enter and leave, and it undoubtedly improves your mood if it is free of clutter. Hooks or a hall tree are needed for coats, hats, and scarves. The area under the stairs is perfect for storage, especially of coats and shoes. It can be left open or shut away behind doors.

Bedrooms

These rooms tend to attract clutter. Keep the bureau and dressing table tidy by putting jewelry and makeup in decorative boxes with lids. If possible, store out-of-season clothes in the attic. There's an enormous variety of fixtures for organizing ties, scarves, socks, and belts that can go inside a wardrobe. Look into what storage systems would fit under the bed: it's a big space. Drawers on casters are easily moved around and very handy as homes for shoes or linen. Baskets make decorative hampers for holding the laundry.

Bathrooms

Usually of limited space, further hindered by piping, bathrooms still must be able to store toiletries, towels, medicines, and cleaning materials. Attractive items like soaps can be displayed on open shelves or windowsills, but you need a cupboard for the rest. Hang laundry bags or multipocketed catchalls on the back of the door. Hang face cloths and bags with bathroom toys from a row of small hooks.

Children's rooms

When working out the storage options here, get down to the child's eye level to identify what looks right. Children's clothes are colorful and attractive, so you could make them a feature and hang them from a pole. The floor space is likely to be a play area, so you want to

DECORATOR'S TIPS

Be creative and find space for storage.

▶ Alcoves are perfect for built-in shelves or closets.

▶ Unused fireplaces can be converted into closets.

▶ Go vertical: high closets are fine for things you don't need ready access to.

▶ No room for a bedside table? Put a small shelf on the wall.

▶ Sliding doors use less space than the hinged variety.

▶ Putting up a partition wall to create storage space can save you money, as you won't need to buy furniture to hold what it stores.

ABOVE Break up the uniformity of row upon row of book spines by including family photographs to make the whole space seem more human. Putting shelves between windows creates pleasing contrast.

RIGHT Varying the size of drawers turns them into an intriguing architectural feature of the room, as here with the small drawer next to the witty carving of a cat.

keep it as clear and open as possible. Raised beds are a popular option here. If you use plastic containers, color code them to identify what goes where.

Work rooms

The first priority is to position essentials like desktop computers near outlets and near a good light source. Have a system for organizing and containing paperwork.

Decorate!

Shelving is a major part of the storage system in your house. It can look great and with careful planning should do a fantastic job keeping your possessions safe, accessible, and tidy. Shelving is easy to assemble and put up, and if your needs change, it is simple to move it elsewhere. Look for areas where shelves could fit easily, such as alcoves, old window spaces, and space on each side of a hearth.

Positioning shelves

Much of it will go along a wall, but start by considering how you will be using your shelving:

Free-standing modular cubed shelving: These can be bought as flat packs or custom-made, and with the right finish, will enhance your living space. Because it is open on both sides, such shelving can be used to delineate areas of the room without closing off any part of it. It can display vases and collections, with books, the telephone, and maybe a wine rack mixed in.

Custom-made shelving: This is another alternative, especially if you want attractive shelving in tricky spaces like under a sloping roof or stairs. One unit could house books, CDs, DVDs, and sound and vision systems. Unsightly elements like the blank TV screen can be concealed behind doors.

Fixed shelving: These types of shelves attach to the wall from L-shaped brackets. These can be made of wood or (more usually) metal, and can be painted to complement your decor. Be clear about what will go on the shelving unit and set the heights of the shelves accordingly. Store matching objects like CDs and DVDs together in shelves of just the right size. A shelf of objects of similar height looks neat and linear: much better than a jumble of odd-sized elements.

Adjustable shelving: This slots or clips into tracks on the wall, so you can adjust the height of each shelf to suit your needs. This might be handy if you keep a lot of books, as they vary in size. Go for deeper, wider-spaced shelves at the bottom for ease of access, and have smaller, closer-spaced shelves higher up.

ABOVE Wicker baskets are an attractive means of storage, and labeling the contents saves a lot of hopeful peering in!

RIGHT Fitted shelving allows you to make the most of the features of a room, such as the display area created in what would otherwise be "dead space" above the window.

PERFECT FINISHES: SHELVING AND YOUR DECOR

▶ Paint your shelves to match or contrast the decorations in the room.

▶ Have curved shelves to soften the line.

▶ Use tapered shelves to add a touch of style.

▶ Glass shelving displays items really well, especially with the right lighting.

▶ Have sections of open shelving broken up by cubes with fitted doors to add variety and visual interest.

Inspirations

Sorting out storage is vital but it can also be frustrating because so many storage methods detract from the look of a room. However, every one of these examples enhances its setting by fitting in yet adding some character of its own.

ABOVE By carving a pattern into the closet doors, then backing them with a bold red accent color, what could be an unsympathetic (but vital) piece of furniture is transformed into a stimulating focal point for the room—and it still stores the glasses!

ABOVE Creating custom-sized storage for your sound system makes it an integral part of the room, not an intrusion.

LEFT Cup hooks turn your drink crockery into a cheery many-contoured feature, so much better than clumsy stacking.

ABOVE If wall space is limited in a bedroom, buy a bed that incorporates drawers underneath the mattress. Such units store a surprising amount of clothes or linen.

LEFT This pretty cupboard can be painted any color to match your decorative scheme, and the handles bring a lovely touch of originality to the room.

CENTER Metal grids have been used to make highly individual shelving that avoids looking too solid and forming a visual block.

▶ A room that is sunny and airy by day might appear not to need much lighting, but by night a flexible scheme is essential for practical and softer lighting.

PAGES 116–117 FOR PLANNING LIGHTING

▶ Lampshades are a crucial finishing touch for many a light fitting. Choose according to your color needs and the room's proportions.

PAGES 120–121 FOR ADJUSTABLE LIGHTS

▶ Adjustable lighting is, by its very nature, extremely flexible as there is so much choice with where it is positioned and the amount of light it emits. Consider combining adjustable with fixed lighting for an even more invigorating light experience.

PAGES 118–119 FOR STYLE CHOICES

LIGHTING

How a room is lit has a huge impact on how it feels, but deciding what your requirements are at different times of day and for different moods is a tricky task—and that is before you look into practicalities and technicalities. Start here, and don't hesitate to get more advice on this complex matter.

Ready?

Lighting plays a vital role in enhancing the decor of every room, yet it needs to be flexible to allow for the various functions a room serves on different occasions and at different times of day. It can be beautiful, too—think of the soft glow of candles, or the sparkle and shimmer of Christmas tree lights. Lighting also sets a mood. If you are able to change the atmosphere in several ways just by altering the lighting, you've got it right. When planning lighting, bear in mind the various types of lighting that you will combine to control the light around your home (see Professional advice, opposite). These will also contribute to the look and feel you want to achieve in each room.

Planning your lighting

Set a mood. The mood you want will alter according to the time of day. During daytime, enhance the natural light with general ambient lighting. In the evening, a softer glow will create an inviting and more intimate feel. You need several separate sources of light for maximum flexibility, and the capacity to dim lights.

Highlight structural elements of the room. What about lighting a beautiful textured beam or a distinctive colored-glass window? Uplights lead the eye upward, making low ceilings appear higher. Downlights will cause shadow above them, lowering the ceiling. Dark ceilings will absorb light. If you paint them white or cream, light will be reflected downward.

Light display cases and closets from the inside, perhaps using different angles to direct attention and also to provide diffused light.

Provide task lighting. Consider which parts of the room need strong light—for example, where you read, sew, or apply makeup.

LIGHTING

PROFESSIONAL ADVICE: TYPES OF LIGHTING

Ambient lighting: This is the general background light. It is calm and neutral, the setting you would use to watch TV. Every room needs some ambient (or mood) lighting.

Accent lighting: Adds interest by highlighting details such as pictures, sculptures, or wall hangings. It's needed most in living rooms and dining rooms.

Task lighting: Allows you to focus on what you're doing, such as reading, cooking, or sewing. You don't want to be distracted, so it must not be harsh, and there should be no glare.

Natural light: Daylight is just as important to a comfortable home environment as electric lights, so allow in as much natural light as possible. One way to lift the gloom in dark corridors is with a light tunnel, which directs natural light from a plastic bubble in the roof down into the gloom. You can also maximize the natural light by partially glazing your external and internal doors.

Candlelight: Nothing can rival the soft, flickering glow of a candle. Everything—faces, glassware, and food—looks better in its atmospheric warmth. Complement candlelight with soft, dimmed lighting and place candles by windows and near mirrors to reflect and enhance the effect.

ABOVE Kitchens in particular benefit from having as much natural light as possible, as it softens the hard lines of equipment and countertops.

LEFT This chandelier provides sculptural interest below the level of the high ceiling, adding a new dimension to the room.

OPPOSITE TOP Lights can be a decorative feature in themeselves, as here with the strings of lights adding depth to the room.

OPPOSITE Matching pairs of lights offer pleasing balance, here enhancing the symmetry of the other furniture and its arrangement.

Set ...

Fixed lights are the ones you can't move, but you can still vary their effects by using different bulbs, shades, or a dimmer switch. You will want to make these adjustments, because nothing is as unflattering to a room than a single source of light blasting out from the middle of the ceiling, completely deadening the atmosphere. Plan lighting well ahead of any other decorating chore, because cables may need to be cut into the walls.

Choose your style

Pendant lights direct light up or down, depending on the shade used. They come in a range of materials—metal for functionality, glass for style, paper for a softer light. The modern take on these is the steel-twist multipendant, which has a terrific artistic quality. Chandeliers have a grand, traditional feel, and can be a sculptural feature. **Wall lights** are usually set at eye level and are an effective source of mood lighting that tends to make the room seem larger, as long as the wall color is suitable (remember, light will bounce off the walls). The light can be diffused in many ways—a gentle pool of light directed upward or a warm glow through tinted glass, for example. Wall fixtures are made in a variety of materials and styles. Plaster ones are made in a neutral color and can be painted to match the wall. Sconces are a traditional style of shaped wall light, usually one or more bulbs on a holder curving out from the wall. **Downlights** shine directional light downward from the ceiling, from a recessed or semirecessed fixture. They can be narrow beam or broad floodlight, and are excellent for taking attention away from a high ceiling. Domed lights can be installed flush or semirecessed and produce highly diffused light. Strip lights provide a broad wash of light, but are not attractive in themselves, so they are often concealed in alcoves or under kitchen cabinets. **Spotlights** can be recessed so they don't disturb the line of the ceiling. They are an effective way of lighting key areas, such as doorways, and can be positioned to make a pleasing pattern. Eyeball spotlights allow you to direct light to the side, maybe to bounce off a wall.

ABOVE Flexibility is so valuable with lighting. This kitchen has lights at different levels to be used practically and esthetically. As the lamps are hidden, the focus is on where the light lands.

LEFT Coloring light softens its impact and allows you to alter the atmosphere in a room. If you can't find shades you like, get in a stock of colored bulbs—then you can change the light as often as you like.

DECORATOR'S TIPS

▶ The light fixture will determine how the light travels.

▶ Omnidirectional light goes in all directions—for example, from a hanging pendant.

▶ Semidirectional light goes mainly in one direction, but a little will diffuse elsewhere—like from a standard lamp.

▶ Directional light is very focused—like the beam from a spotlight.

▶ To see how light will affect different parts of the room, put a table lamp on an extension cable, and position it in different places.

Adjustable lighting

Adjustable lights allow you to change the lighting mood in a room as often as you like. The choice of location is only limited by where the electrical outlets are.

Your choices

Floor lights make a particularly strong style statement in a room. Decide if the room would benefit from having light directed up (to raise the ceiling) or down (maybe as a reading light), or even bounced off the wall. There is a huge variety to choose from, like the timeless French standard lamp or the extremely elegant modern streamlined designs in metal.

Table lights are available in two categories: desk lights and table lamps. Desk lights should be easily adjustable to shine on the task in hand. If the heavy base doesn't appeal to you, try a clamp-on light. Table lamps provide localized lighting, which is also diffused to add to the mood light in a room. The choice of a table lamp is determined by the style of the base (ceramic and wood work well almost anywhere) and of the shade, which can be fabric, glass, or paper. Pairs of table lamps bring unity to your lighting scheme. Placed near a window, table lamps will highlight the textures and colors of curtains.

Track lights allow you to direct a series of lights from a continuous track mounted in the ceiling, and are especially useful in the kitchen. Decide on the beam width you want—a narrow ray to pick out a vase, or a broad splash of decorative light across a collection, or a patterned drape. Another key element to consider when choosing track lighting is the style of the cowl, which can conceal or reveal the bulb.

Uplighters will make the ceiling seem higher, and will produce dramatic shadows if you put plants nearby in the light path. Some also have a spotlight for downlighting. They can also be used as wall lights.

RIGHT Bedside lighting is so important to your comfort and convenience. It needs to be at the right height for reading, and fairly soft so that turning on the light in the night doesn't make you feel as if you are on an airport landing strip.

DECORATOR'S TIPS

▶ The color of the shade will affect the kind of light that is shed, as will the type and color of the bulb.

▶ A lampshade that contrasts strongly with its base makes a big impact.

▶ Shapes cut out of a plain lampshade will add decorative interest to the room and create a novel lighting effect.

▶ Lampshades attract dust: so ensure that you vacuum them regularly.

ABOVE Recessed spotlights are unobtrusive and when combined with well-positioned standard lamps—such as the one to the left of the fireplace—spaces can be delineated very clearly in the evening.

LEFT The beauty of a standard lamp is that is can be moved at will; perhaps brought into a room to help create a different atmosphere when a romantic dinner for two is called for.

Decorate!

Installing lighting is definitely a job for a professional electrician, so here are some ideas for the final decisions and adjustments you may need to make.

Switches

Be flexible. You are bound to want to switch some lights off from different places in your house—the top and bottom of stairwells, for example. So plan ahead for two- and three-way switches. It is also convenient to be able to turn groups of lights off and on, perhaps on entering a living room or bedroom. Use several different circuits and consider using dimmer switches to help make your lighting scheme more flexible.

Bulbs

Fluorescent tubes and spots provide a wash of clear light, which comes close to imitating natural daylight. They are cheap and efficient, but can't be dimmed.

Halogen lamps give bright, very white light. Some low-voltage kinds require a transformer: check with a qualified electrician.

The standard domestic filament lamp (called a tungsten or incandescent lamp) comes in various wattages. They can be silvered internally or on the top to work more like spotlights. Long-lasting, energy-efficient bulbs are well worth the extra money they cost if they are used in locations where replacing the bulb is difficult, for example in a high-hanging pendant.

Mix and match your bulbs. If possible, have a blend of tungsten and halogen lighting so you can mix warm and cool light. Low-wattage bulbs emit a warm, cozy glow—but are hopeless for task lighting. Because bulbs are very easy to change, you could opt for colored bulbs just for the evening when entertaining.

RIGHT Placing a mirror between two sets of candle-effect lights increases the amount of light reflected across the room. Provided it is small, the light source can remain visible and give the impression of a sparkle in the room.

PERFECT FINISHES: LIGHT SWITCHES

If you are making big changes to your lighting arrangements, or are starting from scratch, think about where you want the light switches to be.

▶ They should be at an easy height so that everyone in the house can reach them.

▶ Position the switches near doors so that you can light rooms as you enter them.

▶ There are bound to be some rooms where it would help to have two switches for the same light(s), so that you don't have to cross an unlit room. Bedrooms often need a switch by the door and one by the bed.

▶ Select the switch plates to match your decor. Brass is good for an opulent look, bright primary colors work in a bold scheme.

ABOVE These pleasingly linear light fixtures and hanging lights complement the geometric decorative theme of the room, while lowering the apparent level of the ceiling and providing a choice of lighting for different times and moods.

Inspirations

There are a lot of things to consider when planning lighting. Location, including the height of the lights, is one, but the style of the shades and whether lights need to be placed in pairs are important, too. The shape of the room and how it is used will be your starting point.

ABOVE Choose the right shade for the location. This fur-trimmed shade offers an effective contrast to the plain wall behind.

ABOVE A pull switch really suits the style of this bedside light, with its shade complementing the bedhead shape.

ABOVE The lime green colors and gentle curves of the decor are matched in the chandelier to make the room feel complete. A central hanging fixture like this demands that the focus be in the middle and the layout symmetrical, yet here the effect remains informal.

LEFT These wall lights throw out just the right amount of light for someone reading at one of the chairs, and they act as a frame for the symmetrically mounted set of drawings. This is an example of the placement of lights genuinely enhancing a room setting.

ABOVE This room benefits from interesting lighting at all times of day. During daylight hours the natural light is fully exploited. In the evenings, the low light suspended over the dining table creates a sense of intimacy.

Photography credits

The publisher would like to thank the following photographers for supplying the pictures in this book:

Page 1 Victoria Pearson; **2** Tria Giovan; **3** Edmund Barr; **4 top** David Phelps; **4 bottom** Jacques Dirand; **5 bottom** Fernando bengoechea; **5 top** Nedjeljko Matura; **6** Antoine Bootz; **8** Laura Resen; **9** Thibault Jeanson; **10** Gordon Beall; **11** Marco Ricca; **12 bottom** David Montgomery; **12 top** Tim Beddow; **13 bottom** Tom McWilliam; **13 top** David Montgomery; **14** Pieter Estersohn; **15** Jacques Dirand; **16 bottom** Nancy E. Hill; **16 top** David Phelps; **17** Jacques Dirand; **18** Minh + Wass; **19** Scott Frances; **20 bottom right** Jean-Francois Jaussard; **20 left** Edmund Barr; **20 top right** Oberto Gili; **21** John Ellis; **22** Fernando Bengoechea; **23** Minh + Wass; **24 bottom** Jeff McNamara; **24 top** Joshua McHugh; **25 bottom** Stephen Lewis; **25 top** René Stoeltie; **26** Victoria Pearson; **27** Jacques Dirand; **28** Roger Davies; **29** Fernando Bengoechea; **30** Simon McBride; **32 bottom right** Eric Piasecki; **32 left** Michael Luppino; **32 top right** Pia Tryde; **33** Jonn Coolidge; **34** Toshi Otsuki; **35** Grey Crawford; **36 bottom** Tim Street-Porter; **36 top** Robert Hiemstra; **37 bottom** Fritz von der Schulenburg; **37 top** Laura Moss; **38** David Phelps; **39** Tria Giovan; **40** Peter Margonelli; **41** Tim Street-Porter; **42** Jacques Dirand; **43 bottom** Gabi Zimmerman; **44 bottom right** Tria Giovan; **44 left** Oberto Gili; **44 top right** Jonn Coolidge; **45 bottom** Paul Schlismann; **45 top** Dominique Vorillon; **46** Simon Upton; **47** John Ellis; **49** Laura Resen; **50 bottom** Simon Upton; **50 top** Christopher Drake; **51 bottom** Michael Skott; **51 top** Vicente Wolf; **52** Jacques Dirand; **53** Tria Giovan; **54** Pieter Estersohn; **55** Dennis Krukowski; **56 bottom** Eric Boman; **56 top** Jeff McNamara; **57** Scott Frances; **58 bottom** Scott Frances; **58 top** Gordon Beall; **59 bottom** William Waldron; **59 top** Simon Upton; **60 bottom right** Fritz von der Schulenburg; **60 left** Jonn Coolidge; **60 top right** René Stoeltie; **61 bottom** Oberto Gili; **61 top** Oberto Gili; **62** Nedjeljko Matura; **63** Jacques Dirand; **64 bottom** Oberto Gili; **64 top** Pieter Estersohn; **65 bottom** Gordon Beall; **65 top** Oberto Gili; **66 bottom** Courtesy of *House Beautiful*; **66 top** Victoria Pearson; **67 bottom** Fernando Bengoechea; **67 top** Tim Beddow; **68** John Hall; **70** Laura Resen; **71** Jacques Dirand; **72 bottom** Peter Margonelli; **72 top** Gordon Beall; **73 bottom left** Jonn Coolidge; **73 bottom right** Eric Piasecki; **73 top** Peter Margonelli; **74 bottom right** Grey Crawford; **74 left** Paul Schlismann; **74 top right** Peter Aaron/Esto; **75** Luca Trovato; **76** David Prince; **77** René Stoeltie; **78** Roger Davies; **80 bottom** Guy Bouchet; **80 top** Colleen Duffley; **81 bottom** Victoria Pearson; **81 top** Susan Gentry McWhinney; **82** Jeff McNamara; **83** Tim Street-Porter; **84 bottom** Anne Gummerson; **84 top** Steven Randazzo; **85 bottom** Carlos Domenech; **85 top right** Alan Weintraub; **86 bottom** Michel Arnaud; **86 left** Victoria Pearson; **86 top** Jeff McNamara; **87 bottom** Tom McWilliam; **87 top** Oberto Gili; **88** Jeff McNamara; **89** Fernando Bengoechea; **90 bottom** John Dolan; **90 top** David Hiscock; **91 bottom** Carlos Domenech; **91 top** Gordon Beall; **92** David Hiscock; **93** Andreas von Einsiedel; **94** Oberto Gili; **96 bottom** Colleen Duffley; **96 top** Victoria Pearson; **97 bottom left** Roger Davies; **97 bottom right** Tria Giovan; **97 top** Jonn Coolidge; **98** William P. Steele; **99** Oberto Gili; **100** Fernando Bengoechea; **101** Christophe Dugied; **102 bottom right** Tria Giovan; **102 left** Jeff McNamara; **102 top right** Tria Giovan; **103** David Hiscock; **104** Michel Arnaud; **105** Jonn Coolidge; **106 bottom** Tim Street-Porter; **106 top** David Prince; **107 bottom** Michel Arnaud; **107 top** Toshi Otsuki; **108** Gordon Beall; **109** Victoria Pearson; **110** David Hiscock; **111** Edmund Barr; **112 bottom** Courtesy of *House Beautiful*; **112 left** Oberto Gili; **112 top** William Waldron; **113 bottom right** Fernando Bengoechea; **113 top left** Courtesy of *House Beautiful*; **113 top right** Daniel Piassick; **114** Jonn Coolidge; **115** Eric Roth; **116 bottom** Tria Giovan; **116 top** Thibault Jeanson; **117 bottom** Gordon Beall; **117 top** Victoria Pearson; **118** Thibault Jeanson; **119** Richard Bryant/Arcaid; **120** Jonn Coolidge; **121 bottom** Scott Frances; **121 top** Antoine Bootz; **122** Roger Davies; **123** Eric Piasecki; **124 bottom** Thibault Jeanson; **124 left** Simon Upton; **124 top centre** Antoine Bootz; **124 top right** Antoine Bootz; **125** Oberto Gili.

Index